SANTALI
A Look into Santal Morphology

SANTALI

A LOOK INTO SANTAL MORPHOLOGY

ARUN GHOSH

GYAN

GYAN PUBLISHING HOUSE

NEW DELHI-110 002

Santali: A Look into Santal Morphology

(Language, Linguistics, Tribal Studies, Reference)

ISBN: 9788121204514

Library of Congress Card No. 93-900314

Reprinted in 2018 in India by
Gyan Publishing House
5,Ansari Road, Daryaganj,
New Delhi - 110002
Phones : 011-47034999, 9811692060

e-mail : books@gyanbooks.com
website : www.gyanbooks.com

Dedicated to the Memory of
My Teacher and a Great Soul
Late Professor Dwijendra Nath Basu

FOREWORD

It is highly gratifying to see that a complete work on the descriptive morphology of Santali is ready for presentation to the scholars and discerning readers.

When the founding fathers of our Constitution incorporated a few languages to its Eighth Schedule, thereby assigning a special status to them, they were guided (or misguided even) by the high literary traditions of these languages. The easy assumption at that time was that a highly literate language is a much better language than one with a less developed literature. By 'literature' people also meant literature written, not literature spoken or recited. Oral literature, however rich, was not regarded as literature at all. So Santali, in spite of the numerical strength of its speakers and extremely rich oral tradition, as well as Mundari and others, could not be considered to be a candidate for inclusion in the above Schedule. That a language was basically a tool for communication and only secondarily a vehicle for literature is a perception that was absent in such decision-making process.

Santali, of course, possessed its scripts. It, in fact, has too many of them. Most of them are borrowed from those of the dominating language of the areas where the Santals live, i.e., West Bengal, Bihar and Orissa, including the Roman script, first introduced, as one would expect, by the missionaries from abroad. Borrowal of scripts, of course, is nothing to be touchy about, since it is more the rule everywhere rather than an exception. Santali has also a script devised for itself, which is *OL*, invented by Pandit Raghunath Murmu.

Script or no-script, literature or no literature, if a language is spoken by a sizeable population, it must be important to the administration, since through it the members of the same can reach to more people than through a literate but 'smaller' language. The audio and audio-visual media have made scriptal communication redundant in many areas. Another consideration is that many of the speakers of even the 'literate' languages have themselves remained without letters so long and this has made a mild mockery of the special place of pride for the languages in the Eighth Schedule.

A new look, therefore, at which languages should be included in this schedule, has become an imperative. Nepali, Manipuri, Konkani, etc. are in the process of being incorporated, but the case of Santali, Mundari, etc. should neither be avoided nor delayed. Literature and script have little to do with language and it is time that we do away with our literary bias in judging the efficacy of a language.

One other thing that needs reminding. In dealing with the so-called underdeveloped (or 'developing', if you would insist) languages, one can often fall into the trap of adopting a condescending posture. He considers himself a 'missionary' doing something great to help this 'poor' language, in bringing it out in the sunshine of world attention. The amateurs are the worst offenders here. I have seen books in which Santali has been peddled as a source of all languages of the world and no less. These books do not deserve a mention in any self-respecting and scientifically valid sentence and they ultimately get what they richly deserve, i.e., a place in the oblivion. But not before doing considerable harm by infusing a false sense of superiority to the speakers of the language, on totally unsound grounds. A community's ego, inflated by thin air or vapour supplied by linguistic hacks, can do the community no good.

Which is why such solid scientific works, as done by Dr. Ghosh in the following pages, are needed so much for discovering the real merits of a language. To a non-native learner, Santali morphology is probably the most difficult part of the language and puts an unsurmountable block in the way of learning it. Still, it has its system of patterns and rules, and once these are neatly demonstrated, as they have been by Dr. Ghosh, the distinctive features of the language become accessible to both scholars and ordinary learners.

I have found Dr. Ghosh's work incisive in its attempts at discovery and painstaking in its efforts in collecting and marshalling all the relevant data. I am sure the scholars in the area, as well as those outside, will welcome the publication of this admirable work.

Rabindra Bharati University
Calcutta

PABITRA SARKAR
Vice-Chancellor

PREFACE

The present work is a revised version of my Doctoral dissertation of Calcutta University. The analysis is done on the basis of the data primarily collected through an intensive field survey in the late seventies and early eighties. During revision in the late eighties also field survey was undertaken for clarification of certain points. The survey is carried out only in those areas where the Santals mustered very strong and have been inhabiting for some decades. The Santals of Assam and Tripura are not considered as they are actually taken over as tea plant labourers from either Bihar or West Bengal or from both. The Santals of 24 Parganas or West Bengal are not considered too as they migrate very recently. In doing the survey the blocs are chosen which are inhabited by 20,000 or more Santal speakers. In the process in West Bengal Chatna, Saltora, Khatra, Ranibandh, Raipur, Taldangra and Simlapal blocs in Bankura district, Garhbeta, Shalbani, Jambani, Binpur, Keshiari, Gopiballabhpur, Nayagram and Jhargram blocs in Midnapur, Kashipur and Baghmundi blocs in Purulia, Santal Parganas in Bihar were chosen. After a pilot survey once in West Bengal and once in Bihar a skeleton of possible differences were chalked out and a detailed questionnaire of some six hundred sentences were recorded from the informants of different age and sex groups. In covering the whole six hundred sentences different villages under each bloc were visited and if any difference was noticed with any informant that was verified with other informants.

In 1979 Late Professor D. N. Basu of Calcutta University suggested this topic for my research and guided me until his sudden demise in 1981. His constant encouragement and guidance were the main source of energy behind the work. I record my deep and sincere regards to him. I also record my sincere regards to Professor Chinmoy Dutt who took over as my guide after Professor Basu and led to its successful completion.

I gratefully acknowledge my indebtedness to Professor Pranabesh Sinha Roy who went through an early draft of the work and enlightened me with his valuable comments. During the revision I had very enriching discussions with him which have improved the work to a great extent.

I owe much to Professor K. L. Pike of the University of Michigan, USA, Professor Peter Tradgill, Reading University, U.K., Professor Satya Ranjan Banerjee, Dr. Subhadra K. Sen, and Dr. M.K. Nath of Calcutta University for their constant encouragement.

I take the opportunity to extend thanks to a large number of Santal brethren without whose invaluable assistance in providing data the present work would not have been completed.

I owe much to Professor Pabitra Sarkar, Vice Chancellor, Rabindra Bharati University, Calcutta for engrossing discussions I had with him during revision and for the FOREWORD.

Thanks are also due to the Calcutta University authority who helped in undertaking and completing the project by awarding me the Khaira Research Scholarship and ultimately by conferring on me the Ph. D. degree.

I remember with happiness the moral assistance I received from my teacher Professor Radharaman Chakrabarti, Director, Netaji Institute for Asian Studies, Calcutta, during the revision of the work.

Thanks are due to my friends Gautam and Apurba for their constant insistence on publishing the work. This work would have been impossible without encouragement and assistance from Sri Debidas and Gurudas Bandyopadhyay who not only provided me with a home in the interiors of Bankura during field survey, but also accepted all my demands with a big heart.

I do not find a suitable word to express my feelings for my parents without whose blessings and support, ethereal and practical, I could not continue the work. The work could not see the light of the day had I not got an understanding wife and beloved daughters Mom and Pupul.

My esteemed colleague Smt. Shanti Dutta prepared the whole typescript with great involvement and care. I am grateful to her.

I thank Shri B. P. Garg of Gyan Publishing House for his concern and neat printing of the work.

CONTENTS

1

INTRODUCTION

Santali belongs to the Kherwari group of the North Munda subfamily of the Muṇda family which is, in its turn, a section of the western group of the 'great' Austroasiatic family of languages. Pinnow[1] offered a classification of the Austroasiatic languages into two main branches - West Obergruppe consisting of Munda languages and Nahali[2] and Ost Obergruppe including the rest of the Austroasiatic languages. N.H.Zide (1969) divides the Munda languages into two main groups -- South Munda (abbreviated SM) and North Munda (abbreviated NM). The eastern i.e. Kherwari and the Western i.e. Korku form the North Munda branch. Santali is separated off as a special branch of Kherwari. South Munda, on the other hand, consists of Koraput Munda (abbreviated KM) and Central Munda (abbreviated CM). Koraput Munda consists of Sora-Gorum (abbreviated SG) group and Gutob-Remo-Gaťʼ (abbreviated GRG). Central Munda consists of Kharia and Juang.[3] S. Bhattacharya[4] conforming to the same geographical classification puts forward another classification based on some morphological considerations. He proposes a two-way division—Lower Munda, consisting of the three extreme southern languages Didey (Gta?), Bonda and Gutab spoken in Koraput district of Orissa bordering Andhra Pradesh and Upper Munda covering the rest. As the three southern-most languages included in lower Munda as opposed to the upper Munda, do not show the pronominal incorporation in the verb, differ in respect to genitive marker and by not having the dual marker they are branched off from the rest of the Munda languages. But whatever be the situation, the position of Santali remains the same. Santali has been branched off as a special member of Kherwari (North-eastern) group possibly because it has reached a higher stage of development than any other languages of the same group and also preserves the peculiar linguistic features of Munda more faithfully than the rest.

The name 'Santal' is the anglicized form of *Sãotal*, derived, in turn, from *Sāmanta-pāla*[5] 'dweller of the frontier' and is used to name the tribe by the Bengali. L.P. Skrefsrud[6] tried to derive the same from *Sãot*, a place in Midnapur where the Santals are supposed to have been settled in remote antiquity. There is still a place named *Sãot* in Midnapur where the Santal habitate is very common. But the derivation of *Sãotal* from *Sãot* is nothing but a mere assumption. The Santals call themselves *hor* 'man' and the name Santal is only used by those who are Christianised. From the term *mañjhi* or *mãjhi* 'village head man' they also call themselves *manjhi* or *majhi* when asked about their caste. Being the oldest ethnic stock in India, they are also known as *adivasi* 'those who have been living in the land from the very beginning'. S.K. Chatterji[7] attaches great importance to this name remembering the contribution of the Santals in the evolution of Indian life and culture.

Santali, the language name, is derived from the ethnic name. From *Sãotal*, the Bengali use the name *Sãotali* for their language. The Santals themselves call their language *hoṛ* or *hoṛ roṛ*, being more analytical, *roṛ* 'language, speech' is attached to *hoṛ* 'Santal, man', hence 'language of the Santals'. The language is also sometimes returned under the name *mãjhi bhasa* 'language of the *mãjhi*.' In North Bengal the language is known as *jaṅli* or *paharia*. In the South Bengal and Orissa, the language is known as *ṭhaṛ*, in Bihar it is named as *parsi* 'foreign'.

The Santal population is spread over a large strip of land covering almost the whole of eastern India—say, West Bengal, Bihar, Orissa and Assam. The most compact area of Santal population comprises the West of Birbhum and Burdwan, the sadar sub-division of Bunkura, the Jhargram sub-division of Midnapur, almost the whole of Púrulia, in West Bengal; the south of Bhagalpur and Monghyr, the Santal Parganas, Hazaribagh and Dhalbhum in Bihar and Baleshwar and Mayurbhanj and Keonjhar in Orissa. In Assam the Santal settlements are confined to tea gardens only, where they migrated and still migrate for the purpose of having occupation in the tea plants. Their scattered settlements are also found in North Bengal, South 24 Parganas, Hooghly, Howrah etc. in South Bengal where they are occupied as day-labours. The Santals settled at Rajsahi, Rangpur and Chittagong hill tracts in Bangladesh are not the natives of its soil. They are all immigrants. They had migrated from India at different periods.

The total number of the Santals according to mother tongue speakers, in India is, according to 1991 Census, 4,332,511 of which 1,632,440 is in West Bengal, 2,161,032 in Bihar, 529,574 in Orissa, 86,303 in Assam and a few thousands in Tripura and Madhya Pradesh.[8]

The distribution of the Santals in different States are as follows :

Speakers of Languages/Mother Tongues

State	*Total*	*Male*	*Female*
Andhra Pradesh	50	30	20
Bihar	2,161,032	1,087,820	1,073,212
Gujarat	40	30	10
Haryana	10	5	5
Himachal Pradesh	7	7	-
Jammu & kashmir	28	26	2
Karnataka	45	30	15
Madhya Pradesh	715	445	270
Maharashtra	110	64	46

Manipur	351	348	3
Meghalaya	212	199	13
Nagaland	1,100	1,080	20
Orissa	529,574	264,854	264,718
Punjab	10	10	-
Rajasthan	52	37	15
Sikkim	16	14	2
Tripura	3,508	1,812	1,696
Uttar Pradesh	282	257	25
West Bengal	1,632,440	822,973	809,467
Andaman & Nicobar Islands	7	3	4
Arunachal Pradesh	484	282	202
Chandigarh	10	8	2
Delhi	126	69	57
Goa, Daman & Diu	1	1	-
Mizoram	2,301	2,278	23

The Santals are the most numerous among the tribes who speak Munda. In western fringe of West Bengal, north Orissa and Santal Parganas, normally, they muster very strong and this helps them maintaining group solidarity and preserve their language and culture much better than elsewhere. But elsewhere, the Santals now remaining, are but like scattered remnants of a substance floating here and there in a mass of water, into which they have been all but melted and in which they are on the point of disappearing. By far, the greater part of their substance has already commingled in the fluid around them, the remainder is saturated with it and it is only in the very kernel and inner centre of the largest lumps, that something, like thc pure original substance is to be sought. They are found whereever a bunch of hills or an unhealthy jungle has given them refuge. Even there, they are closely surrounded by, and to a considerable extent penetrated, or saturated with an Aryan element which modifies both their features and their language.

The proportion of the population retaining the Santali language decreases as the tribe spreads out to industrial and more accessible areas. For example, in West Bengal as a whole, 55% of the Santals speak their own language but in 24-Parganas the proportion falls to 10%. The total number of bilinguals among the Santals is 1,501,638, i.e. 34.66% of the total.[9]

The bilingualism is more extensive among the tribal population than among the general population. While the national average of bilingualism is 13.34%, it is more than 30% in case of the tribal population.[10] Obviously, the necessity for knowing the most common language of the area is very great in the case of the tribes who speak the tribal language which is obviously, a minority one. As a rule, bilingualism is encouraged whenever a small linguistic group finds itself planted in the midst of a population speaking a different tongue.

It is worth mentioning that the Santal speech community is scattered among a number of political units, some members of it permanently belonging to West Bengal, some to Bihar, some to Orissa and some elsewhere. Their original habitat still remains undeciphered. As it is not still included in the 8th schedule as an official language of a political unit, unlike the Aryan and Dravidian speech communities they don't have 'terra firma' under their heel. The study of their language in different areas is needed as they are mostly bilinguals. Being a minority speech community, they cannot help speaking the dominant language of the region where they stay. In everyday interaction, they have to come across a group of people who belong to a different speech community viz. Bengali speech community in West Bengal, Bihari speech community in Bihar, Oriya in Orissa, Assamese in Assam. So it is very common that the local languages will influence their native tongue — somehow or other. In this way Santali is to some extent, modified in phonology, morphology, syntax and vocabulary. The lexical items of the local languages are taken into Santali with some nativizing elements or as they are. The connotation of some lexical items is changed under the influence of the neighbouring languages. The new suffixes and postpositions are borrowed and nativized following the phonotactic rules of its own. The influence of its neighbouring languages in syntax remains to be seen. The extent of influence on Santali vocabulary and grammar may be shown with certain examples.

As they grow more civilized they start adopting Aryan systems along with designations for the same : thus *ladu* 'cakẹ', *mithai* 'sweet', *dal* 'beans', *caole* 'rice' *panahi* 'shoes' & c. Specialized crafts originally do not belong to them and as the shoemaker, blacksmith, carter do not belong to the Santal society the corresponding terms like *muci* 'shoemaker', *kamar* 'blacksmith', *gadvan* 'carter' are borrowed from Aryan. Similarly, trade not belonging to their regular means of livelihood, the trade terms like *mal* 'goods', *cij* 'sample', *asbab* 'furniture', *bajar* 'market', *kh rca* 'expense' are taken from or through the neighbouring Aryan languages. In time calculation the Aryan influence is noticeable : thus we have *ghari* 'a while', *din* 'day', *b ch r* 'year', *cir kal* 'a long time'. Even though they have got their own village administration the Aryan terms like *manjhi* or *majhi* 'headman' (Skt. madhya), *pancayat* are used. Even in the household the Aryan influence is clear. The inner appartment is *bhitar* or *bhitri*, door is *duar*. The terms like *pukhri* 'pond', *bande* 'id' are of Aryan origin. Normally, the kinship terms and the terms for the body parts of any language are kept free from foreign influence. But here, the Aryan influence is so strong that the kinship system is also affected. Thus wife is *babu*, nephew *bhagna*, niece *bhagni*, *bh i* is brother. The terms for the sentimental feelings are borrowed from Aryan : thus *maya* 'affection', *daya* 'pity', *laj* 'shame'

In the grammatical level, like the lexical one, the Aryan influence is fast progressing. The grammatical gender, though attested only in a few examples, is framed on the analogy of Aryan, the masculine nouns being ended with /-a/ and feminine /- i/; thus *kala* 'deaf' masc. and *kali* 'id' feminine; *kora* 'boy, young man', masc. *kuri* 'girl, young lady' fem. The first three ordinal numbers *pahil-poilo*, *d sar* and *tesar* are borrowed from Hindi. A good number of postpositions like *lagit* 'for', *a nge* 'along with', *upar* 'above' *bhitābhitri* 'inside', *sathe* 'with' & c. are borrowed from Aryan either through Hindi or Bengali. The particles like *judi-jodi* 'if', jɛ*m n* 'so that', *tahle* 'for that', *to, ar* 'and' *t kh n* 'then' & c are from the same source. In verb also very many Aryan roots like *cal* 'go', *bujh* 'understand' are borrowed, but with modification, here / -ao / or / -au / are added resulting in *calao, bujhau*. But when they are conjugated the verbal suffixes are indigenous. Aryan nouns are used as verbs but are so nativized that they fit well to the Santali pattern. In *bahu-ad-e-a-n* 'I gave him a wife', *bida - ka -e -a -ko* 'they sent him off', the Aryan nouns *bahu* and *bida* are pitted against the Santali suffixes.

In Santali, though the influence of the neighbouring Indo-Aryan languages is strongly felt in modern times than before, the grammar is not so much exposed as the vocabulary. And the non-native elements which are getting their way into the language are being readily nativized by giving a phonetic twist and thus they are well incorporated in the language. In the non-native elements, following the native pattern the vowel/a/ is neutralised if it is preceded or followed by i or u : thus *bhitar* for *bhitar*, *kali* for *kali*, *kami* for *kami*, *juan* for *joan* or *juan*, *bahu* for *bahu*, *pachim* for *pachim*, *caukidar* for *caukidar*, *upar* for *upar*, *sutam* for *suta* 'thread', *mandir* for *mandir* 'temple', *laḍu* for *laḍḍu* 'sweet meat', *sari* for *sari* 'saree', *rani* for *rani* 'queen', *thai* for *thai* 'place', *utar* for *uttar* 'north', *rai* for *rai* 'mustard', *lagit* 'for *lagi*, *mami* for *mami* maternal aunt' & c. The borrowed verb roots are nativized by replacing the final/a/ with/ao/or/au thus *paṛao* 'to fall', *calao* 'to go', *bujhau* 'to understand' *j rao* 'to link', *laga* 'to cultivate' & c. The borrowed words or grammatical elements ending in a vowel are added with a checked consonant in the final position : thus, / *'lagit'* / 'for'/ -ṭak'/ definite article.

Santali being scattered in different places is subject to differences in phonology, morphology and vocabulary. Considering that there has been no settled standard, R.N. Cust mentioned of four dialects which, according to him, was not improbable.[11] Although four dialects are not attested, a line of demarcation is emerging gradually between Santali spoken in the districts of Midnapore, Purulia and south Bankura comprising Khatra, Ranibandh, Raipur, Taldangra and Simlipal blocks in West Bengal and Baleshwar, Mayurbhanj and Keonjhar in Orissa and that spoken in north

Bankura comprising Chhatna and Saltora blocks, Birbhum, Malda, West Dinajpur and Jalpaiguri in West Bengal, Santal Parganas, Bhagalpur, Munghyr in Bihar. Campbell[12] mentioned these two dialects and named them Southern and Northern dialects respectively. For certain practical hazards, having in our survey, all the areas mentioned by Campbell are not undertaken. Covering only West Bengal and Santal Parganas of Bihar dialectal situation in Santali has been chalked out and in that case also Campbell's demarcation as Northern and Southern has been conformed. As already remarked the dialects are still in the process of formation and the differences between the two is not great. Certain differences between the two dialects, Northern, (henceforth N.S.) and Southern (henceforth S.S.) are the following :

In phonology, the southern dialect is more simplified than the northern one.

In the southern dialect, the pronunciation of /a/ is gradually missing which is being replaced by /a/; the northern dialect, on the other end, still clings to this.

Loss of homorganic nasal and nasalization of the preceding vowel is another feature of the southern one, compare —

Southern	Northern
põṛ	*ponḍ* 'white'
mãjhi	*mañjhi* 'village headman'
aṛia	*anḍia* 'male cow'
bhĩdar	*bhindar* 'to fall'
adon	*andok* 'to come out'
cãdo	*cando* 'sun'

In case of *nondE* 'here' *ndE* 'there yonder' the nasal is slightly heard.

Pronunciation of post alveolar stop as flap is more or less a common feature of the southern dialect. Compare —

Southern	Northern
põṛ	*ponḍ* 'white'
baṛa	*baḍa* 'to know'

huṛin	*hudin* 'younger'
gEṛE~gEḍE	*gEḍE* 'Sean'
bheṛa~bheḍa	*bheḍa* 'ram'

nonḍE, onḍE and *hanḍE* are also sometimes heard as *noṛE, oṛE* and *haṛE* respectively.

There is a preference for nasal in the southern dialect as compared with the northern which preserves the checked stops. Compare —

Southern	Northern
/-aṅ /	/-ak'/ genetive suffix
/-rEaṁ/	/-rEak'/ do
/-ṭaṅ/	/-ṭak'/ enclitic definitive
/-sEn /	/-sEc' / 'towards'.

In the southern dialect there is also a tendency, although shared by the younger generation of the northern dialect, of pronouncing /e/ as [i] and /o/ as [u]. In certain examples the pronunciation of /e/ as [i] and /o/ as [u] has been established; e.g. *abin* 'you two' (cp. *aben* in N.S.), *unku* 'they' (cp. *onko* in N.S.) ni 'this' (cp. *ne* in N.S.).

In morphology the southern dialect shows some peculiarities compared with the northern one.

In the genitive case, two suffixes are used when the governed noun is animate, one for the singular and the other for the plural. /ic'/ is added when the governed noun is singular and /- rEn/ when it is plural. In the northern dialect, on the other hand, /-rEn/ is used for singular and plural both (vide ch.III).

In the causative-permissive verb stem the formative is /-hoc / in the southern dialect and /-oco/ in the northern.

In vocabulary, the southern and the northern dialects are different, initiated by borrowings from the neighbouring languages. The local borrowings in the two dialects is so high that it has made one almost unintelligible to the other. In certain cases the usage is also different. The terms like *Eṅga* 'mother', *Era* 'wife', *hErEl* 'husband' etc. are treated as vulgar in the southern dialect and are almost obsolete, while in the northern they are regularly used in the aforesaid sense. They are, in the southern dialect, are replaced by *ayo* 'mother', *bahu* 'wife' and *jãvãy* 'husband' respectively. The same thing is sometimes indicated by different terms, for instance, 'cloth' is *lugri* in the southern and *kicric'* in the northern, 'shirt' is *dɔtɔ* in the southern and *jama* in the northern.

Santali was first brought to light by the foreign missionaries. Prior to that no attempt had been made to study this language by any Indian. Although there seemed to have a suppressed motivation of exploiting these simple and ignorant people. "Far from the maddning crowd's ignoble strife" they led a life quite ignorant of the civilized world. They did not have a square deal from any corner. And this was the condition which led the Europeans to work among them. It may not be true that some of them were employed by the British rulers in India to wash the brain of the Santals which would positively help the rulers to rule over them. But it still remains unquestionable that the missionaries were the first to bring Santali into the knowledge of the world and to make it accessible to the scholarly world.

Rev. J. Phillips (1845) was the pioneer among the European scholars in throwing light on the Santali language in his *A Santali Primer.*[13] In 1850 his *Sequel to A Santali Primer*[14] appeared. Both the works, though the latter one can be said to be supplementary to the earlier one, brought sensation in the scholarly world. In his *An Introduction to the Santal Language* (1852)[15] we find a comprehensive grammar, although in the *Preface* he recognized the limitations about giving any very accurate account of the numbers and language spoken by the Santals for the limited acquaintance with them. In his *Introduction* he submits with "unfeigned diffidence" : ".... A first effort, ...; is necessarily exposed to many errors, which time and careful observation alone can correct. In the absence of all established authority, much difficulty has been experienced in fixing the orthography, and ascertaining the exact meaning of many words, as they are differently used and differently pronounced by different persons." As Santali has no characters of its own "to supply this deficiency the Bengali alphabet has been adopted" (p-1). The palatal nasal /ñ/ is identified as velar nassal, represented by Bengali. No distinction has been made among the checked consonants. All are represented by : (visarga). Among other things the derivative nouns have been paid attention. Santali verb being the most complicated one has been paid much attention. Some 39 pages have been devoted to verb (p.13-51) as compared with other chapters, of chapter I (OF Letters) pp. 1-3, Chapter V (OF Adjectives, Adverbs & c) pp. 51-57. (It consists of two parts- Grammar (p. 1-57) and Reading Lessons (58-82). At the end, Vocabulary (p. 83-186) enters.

Rev. L.O. Skrefsrud's *A Grammer of the Santal Language* (1873)[16] is the first authoritative and comprehensive study of the Santali language although he has adopted the old name Turanian as the ultimate source of the language. The grammar is divided into two parts — the first part discussing phonology and morphology, although not named as such and the second part discussing syntax. The short and long counterparts of the seven vowels, viz. a, e, e, i, o, o and u are mentioned and the neutral vowels a, i, o and u are first posed. Here, also, the checked consonants k', c; (represented ch'), t' and p' were first recognized and described. The pronunciation of all the "letters" are given by comparing them with German or English equivalents. The conditions under which the four checked consonants are changed to their corresponding full voiced counterparts are discussed in the section "of the permutation of letters" (Ch. I : Sec IV). Like Phillips three methods of noun declenseon — one belonging to Masculine-Feminine and the other two to Neuter, are discussed (Ch. II). The possessive pronouns which are actually suffixed forms of the personal pronouns are also classed with the personal, demonstrative and interrogative pronouns as a separate entity (Ch. IV). The number of the demonstrative is not so large as mentioned by P.O. Bodding (1929). Santali verb morphology is of the greatest complexity and that Skrefsrud had felt it well, can be seen from the range of discussion — while the entire phonology and morphology have been accomodated in 40 pages (sounds pp. 1 - 2 and morphology pp. 3- 40) the verb is given some 255 pages (pp.40-295). The stem discussed in the present thesis as benefactive is discussed by Skrefsrud as reservative. His elaborate discussion of verbs has made it more complex. The derivation of nouns from nouns, adjectives, verbs and adverbs by suffixation, infixation and compounding is discussed in detail (Ch. VII : 303-326).

Before G. A. Grierson (1906) and P.O. Bodding (1922-29), Rev. F.T. Cole attempted in his *Santali Primer* (1896)[17] "to clear up some of the difficulties experienced by beginners in their first efforts to acquire their difficult and idiomatic language" (*Preface*). It consists of 55 chapters. The verb is discussed in detail (pp. 37-95) with remark, "The wonderful intricacy of the verbal system is a marvel to the student and considering the mental calibre of the Santals of the present day, one is all the more surprised to find such a complex, and yet perfectly regular, verbal system" (p.37). It may be called a simplified version of Skrefsrud.

G.A. Grierson as a part of his survey of the Indian languages has touched upon the Munda languages, especially Santali in his *Linguistic Survey of India* Vol. IV (1906)[18]. Along with discussing the sounds and grammatical features, he has given a skeleton grammar in a tabular form in which nouns, pronouns, "conjugational bases" (Vol. IV : 53) inlexional bases (IV : 53) and negative particles are entered. The description of the sounds is phonemic. The different values of E and O are mentioned. Unlike the previous grammars, he has recognized no real cases in Santali. Difference of demonstratives based on proximity and distance are classified. Demonstratives like lateral and intensive and those referring to sight and sound are classified. The finite /a/is mentioned in the Survey as "categorical a" (p.45). Lastly, he has recognized locality-based differences in the language, and that has in recent years given rise to a slight difference in dialect between the east, where most loan words come from Bengali, and the west which chiefly borrows from Bihari, and the south where the influence of Oriya is felt" (p. 54).

P.O. Bodding's *Materials For A Santali Grammar* Pt. I & II (1922; 1929)[19] was the first monumental and most authentic of the grammars written so far and still remains unsurpassed. Living more than three decades among the Santals he grasped the very essence of the language which helped him much in writing the grammar. He was not much satisfied with terminology adopted by him and he submits in the *Foreword* : "..... The working of an agglutinating language or of the mind of the speakers of such a language is, as will be seen, very different from that of an inflexional language. The ordinary grammatical terms have (with a few additions) been used; these are not, however, adequate to the needs of a language that represents a stage of development different from that of the inflexional languages. Any one who could coin terms suitable for the needs of an agglutinating language would render a real service to the student of this and similar languages". All the sounds are correctly described; stress, syllabification and euphonic harmony are studied with minute observations. He has objected to the term neutral used by Skrefsrud and given the conditions under which those vowels are made such. In the part of morphology (named Mostly Morphological) "much syntactic matter has come in, partly because omission would make it more difficult for the student to understand the peculiar working of this agglutinating language" (*Preface*). Different grammatical classes are discussed; his elaborate discussion of the animate - inanimate distinction will remain as the best guide for those who want to study the Santal mental make up for many years to come. The case is not recognized. The section on the postposition is the most elaborate one covering both the native and borrowed ones. His minute observation on different suffixes and detailed discussion of the different types of demonstratives demand special mention. The verb (pp. 164-287) which was made unnecessarily complex by Skrefsrud is made simple and accessible. Had he not died earlier he could have completed the proposed part of syntax. Yet the work done by him in the field of Santali linguistics is still unsurpassable and the future scholars will remember him with reverence. His, *A Santali Grammar For Beginners* (1929)[20] is a concise and simplified version of his *Materials For A Santali Grammar* for the learners. His *A Santal Dictionary* 1-5 (1929-36)[21] remains the best source of expressive derivation.

In the very preface of his *An Introduction to Santali* Pt. I & II, R.M.Macphail submits,[22] "As its name implies, this book does not pretend to be a full grammar. Such a work already exists, in Bodding's *"Materials For a Santali Grammar"*, Parts I and II but that is not an easy book for the beginner, and the need has been felt for something simpler. This is an attempt to meet that need" (*Preface*). It is divided into two parts — the first describing different sounds in Chapter I sets forth some common words and simple constructions in a series of lessons in Chapter II and thereafter describes various grammatical classes using phrases learned in Chapter II to illustrate their use and the Part II consists of a vocabulary of about eleven hundred common Santali words followed by an English-Santali section. It is actually meant for helping the new learners of Santali to find easily how the different forms and functions are formalized. Since it is primarily meant for pedagagical purpose, theoretical discussions and justifications are kept at minimum.

The present analysis is done on the basis of the data primarily collected through an intensive field survey between October 1979 and July 1982 in the bloc level of different districts of West Bengal and Bihar. The data consist of about six hundred sentences, fifteen texts and a few hundreds of words and paradigms.

The survey is carried out only in those areas where they muster very strong and have been inhabiting for a considerable period of time. The Santali of Assam and Tripura are not considered as they are actually taken over as plantation labourers from either Bihar or West Bengal or from both. The Santals of 24 Parganas of West Bengal are not considered either, as they migrated very recently from the aforesaid areas. The survey in Orissa and other districts like Bhagalpur, Hazaribagh, Monghyr, Singhbhum etc. in Bihar was not undertaken for time factor and also for the present work was not primarily intended for dialect survey. For the description of the morphological structure of the language the area actually covered was found sufficient.

In doing the survey the blocs are chosen which are inhabited by 20,000 or more Santal speakers. In this way in West Bengal, Chhatna, Saltora, Khatra, Ranibandh, Raipur, Taldangra and Simlapal blocs in Bankura, Garhbeta, Shalbani, Jambani, Binpur, Keshiary, Gopiballavpur, Nayagram and Jhargram in Midnapur, Rampurhat in Birbhum, Balurghat in West Dinajpur, Kashipur and Baghmundi in Purulia and Santal Parganas in Bihar were chosen. After a pilot survey, once in West Bengal and once in Bihar a skeleton of possible differences were chalked out and a detailed questionnaire was prepared for detailed survey. Following the questionnaire, some six hundred sentences were recorded from the informants of different age and sex either in tape or in writing. The number of words varied in different blocs from time to time. In recording the whole six hundred sentences different villages under each bloc were visited and if any difference was noticed with any informant that was verified by other supporting sentences with other informants. The processing of the material went hand in hand with the survey so that check and feed process could be applied.

Besides this, some published works like that of Skrefsrud (1873), Bodding (1929), Macphail (1953) and a few periodicals like *Pachimbangla* (published by West Bengal Government) were of much help in supplying data.

The present work presents in a fairly exhaustive manner the essential details about the morphological structure. In describing the morphological pattern of nouns, adjectives and adverbs syntax has automatically come in. The animate-inanimate distinction is quite impossible unless syntax is considered. The description of the particles remains incomplete if their syntax is not looked into. The expressive derivation which is developed to a high degree in Santali has been discussed in a fairly detailed way. The complex verb structure is discussed in a simplified manner.

The grammatical classes established on the morphological and syntactic criteria are the following : Nominal including noun and pronoun, verb, adjective and numeral, adverb and particles. Nominal and verb enter into morphological construction while the others do not. In that respect they may be grouped together as one class. But that is avoided on account of their different syntactic behaviour and are treated separately.

The morphological processes employed are prefixation, infixation, suffixation, reduplication and compounding of which the first one is very rare. Compounding involves two root morphemes and in that sense compounding at its purest clashes with derivation which shows an interplay of a root morpheme and a grammatical morpheme. But here compounding is not treated separately and is included in derivation as compound forms are not numerous. When the roots or the root and the affix come together morphonemic changes occur, but that is not of high degree. So without ascribing separate chapter on morphophonemics the changes are treated along side the elements which show such changes in a different sub-section.

Notes on Phonology

Phonemic Inventory

The phonemes of Santali are tabulated below. The phonetic labels give a fair indication of the value in most cases. Differences if any are mentioned simultaneously.

VOWELS :	Front	Central	Back
High	i		u
Mid high	e		o
Mid low	E Ẽ		
Loe		a ã	

Front vowels are unrounded while the back and central ones are rounded. There is no long counterpart of any vowel. Although /E/ and /o/ become /e/ and /ɔ/ respectively when they are preceded or followed by /i/ or /u/, they maintain their distinction when no such condition occurs. The mid-low central [ə] is the neutralised counterpart of /a/ when it is preceded or followed by /i/ or /u/. In transcription [ə] has been retained as the condition in some cases is not apparent, as in Indo-Aryan loan words, e.g. *dəṛ* 'run', *əd* 'beginning', *ət* 'opportunity', *ghəṭ* 'fault', *raska* 'rejoice', *jət* 'caste', *Khəcląk* 'basket', *pəc'* 'recede', *rər* 'tune' etc.

Vowels are not used extensively in initial position All vowels occur in all positions, except [ə] which occurs finally very rarely.

There are a number of vowel sequences occuring medially and finally ; oa, ae, iu, ea, ua, oi, əi, io, ao, ui, ei, ɔe. Of the three vowels sequences only eae is found.

Of the nasal vowels /ã/, /Ẽ/ and /ɔ̃/ are found, while /ã/ occurs in all positions, /Ẽ/ and /ɔ̃/ occur medially and finally.

Consonant :

	Bilabial	Dental	Post-Alveolar	Palatal	Velar
VL	p	t	ṭ	c	k
Vd.	b	d	ḍ	j	g
Nasal	m	n		ñ	ṅ
Frictive		s			h
Flap		r	ṛ		
Lateral		l			
Frictionless continuant				y	

The stops are always unaspirated, aspirates if occur are in loan words but never in final position. The bilabial, dental, palatal and velar stops are unreleased in final position, although in recent loans velar stops maintain its release finally. The post-alveolar stops are released in all positions. For unreleased counterparts /p'/, /t'/, /c'/ and /k'/ are transcribed and maintained throughout the text as a tremendous sentiment of the Santals is involved in it.

Among nasals /ṅ/ does not occur initially while /m/, /n/ and /ñ/ are frequent in all positions. Fricatives do not occur finally. The consonant cluster is rare.

References

1. Pinnow in his latter papers took up the position of the Munda languages and comparing the external relationship of the Munda languages with other Austroasiatic ones he revised his earlier classification slightly, but the position of the Munda remains the same, i.e. Munda-Nahali is separated off as the Western branch; Cf H.J. Pinnow's (1960, 1963) Uber den Ursprung der voneinan der abweichenden Strukturen der Munda Und Khmer - Nikobar Sprachen. *Indo-Iranian Journal* 4, 81-103. The position of the Munda languages within the Austroasiatic family. Linguistic Comparison in South-East Asia and the Pacific, ed. by H.L. Shorto, 140-152.

2. Here the name conforms to that of Robert Shaffer (1940), F.B.J. Kuiper (1962) and S. Bhattacharya (1957) rather than to H.J. Pinnow's (1959) Nihali.

3. Zide's diagram appears thus :

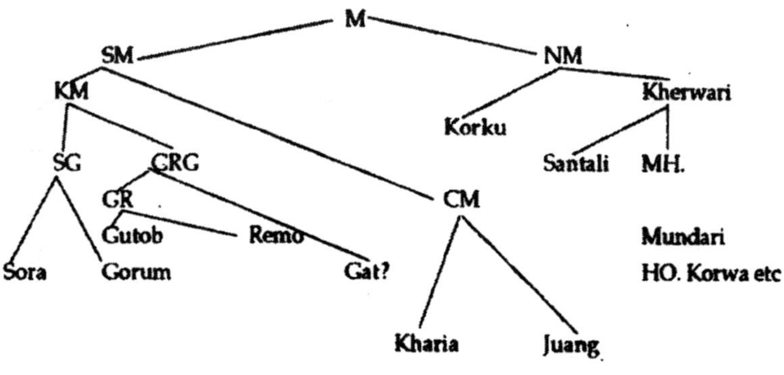

Cf Munda Studies : A New Classification of Munda. *Indo- Iranian Journal*, V.XVII : 1, 1975, pp. 97-101.

4.

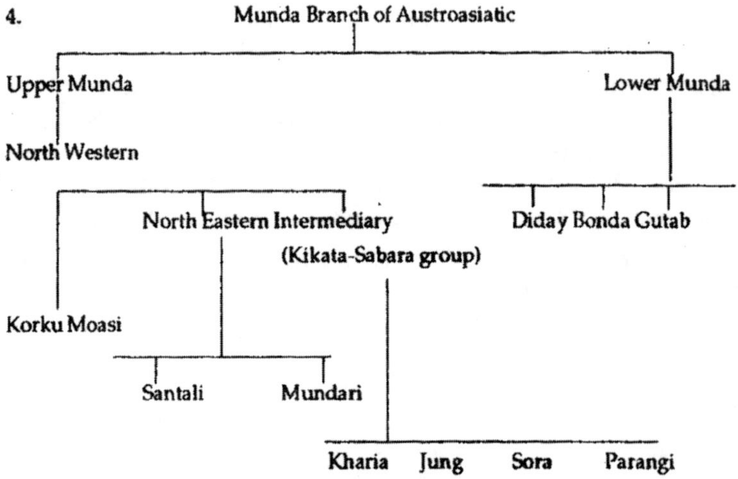

Cf. Munda and Non-Munda Austroasiatic Languages. In : T.A. Sebeok (ed), Current Trends in Linguistics, v.5, pp.411-33. The Hague : Mouton.

5. S.K. Chatterji, FOREWORD to HOR BAPLA PUTHI (Pahil hatin) by Stemphen H. Murmu. Benagaria : Mission Press. pp.V-XI, 1961.
6. L.O. Skrefsrud, A Grammar of the Santhal Language. Benares : Medical Hall Press. 1873, (Introduction).
7. S.K. Chatterji, *op.cit.*
8. Census of India, 1981, Series 1, INDIA-Part IV-B (i), Population by Language / Mother Tongue (Table/C-7). New Delhi : Registrar General and Census Commissioner, India,. The figure given under Assam is according to 1971 Census, as census in 1981 could not be undertaken in Assam due to ethno-political turmoil.
9. Ibid. Part IV-B(ii), Population by Bilingualism (Table C-8), p.4.
10. Ibid. p.5.
11. R.N. Cust, A Sketch of the Modern Languages of the East Indies, London : Trubner, 1878.
12. A. Campbell, Santali-English Dictionary (3rd edn), edited by R.M. Macphail. Benagaria : Santal Christian Council. 1953 (Introduction).
13. J. Phillips, A Santali Primer, Calcutta : School Book Society, 1845.
14. J.Phillips, Sequel to A Santali Primer, Calcutta : School Book Society, 1850.
15. J. Phillips, An Introduction to the Santal Language, Calcutta : School Book Society, 1852.
16. L.O. Skrefsrud, A Grammar of the Santhal Language. Benares : Medical Hall Press, 1873.
17. F.T. Cole, Santali Primer, Pokhuria : Santal Mission Press, 1896.

18. G.A. Grierson, Linguistic Survey of India, V. IV, ed. by Sten Konow, Calcutta : Superintendent of Govt. Printing, 1906.
19. P.O. Bodding, Materials for a Santali Grammar, Part I (Mostly Phonetic) 1922 and Part II (Mostly morphological) 1929. Dumka : Santal Mission of the Northern Churches.
20. P.O. Bodding, A Santali Grammar for Beginners, Benagaria : Santal Mission Press, 1929.
21. P.O. Bodding, A Santal Dictionary, V.1-5, Oslo : A.W. Braggers Boktrykkeri, 1929-36.
22. R.M. Macphail, An Introduction to Santali, Calcutta : Firma KIM, 1983 (Reprint).

2

DERIVATION

Derivation, by definition, is one of the analytical processes which show the combination of the roots with different grammatical morphemes, or with different roots which help expanding the existing volume of the lexicon of the language, and that of course, with the goal of expressing something more which cannot be expressed through the existing resources. In Santali, such expansions occupy a major part in the lexicon.

The phenomenon of derivation is here handled strictly in the sense used by Mathews[1] which suggests 'that branch of lexical morphology which is concerned with formations other than those of compounds'[2], brassing aside, at least for the time being, controversy regarding domain of application of the concept of derivation. The patterns of derivation suggested for Santali derived forms must not be misconstrued as word formation rules of Santali, in order to predict, or constrain, the production of vocabulary items. The patterns are suggested on the basis of data from the author's field notes. They may have exceptions. And if it is assumed 'human beings have creative intelligence which allows them to find non-standard solutions to problems outside language' it is reasonable to suppose that 'at least some cases of linguistic innovation are to be explained as the product of this general intelligence applied to language'[3]. Again atleast some examples of innovations are isolated and elude any particular pattern. Sometimes even an unproductive pattern may be productive in course of time and vice versa. And this is bound to happen if the process of derivation is regarded as a diachronic one.

Santali employs various morphological processes for derivation, viz., prefixation, infixation, suffixation and compounding. Besides morphological processes employed in derivation, there exists another process which consists of shifting certain words from one form-class to another without any apparent application of the morphological devices, which process may be termed as internal derivation as opposed to the external which is manifested by various external devices. The different types of derivation can be shown as follows :

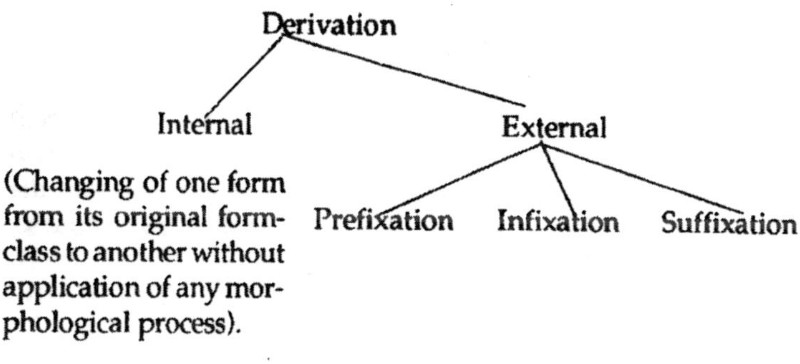

Internal derivation :

Santali strongly favours this process over the pondrous derivatives - polisyllabic and sometimes fraught with morphophonemic complication. In this device the words are spontaneously transmuted from one form-class to another and then the context alone shows whether a noun or adjective or verb is involved. In this way, many words, in Santali, have the potential capacity of being used as noun, adjective or verb, the context alone determines which part of speech is to be used to express what the word conveys. For example -

kombro straddles the domain of noun, i.e. thief -

komoro ñir-en-a-e 'the thief ran away', adjective, i.e. thieving, bereft of or stolen - *kombro hoṛ* 'thieving person' or 'bereft person', *kombro mErOm* 'a stolen goat' and verb i.e. steal *mErOm-ko kombro-ked-e-a* 'they steal the goat', *noa dokombro-an-a* 'this (inanimate) was stolen'. Similarly, *oṛak'* can be used as noun i.e. house - *uni oṛak'-rE mena-e-a* 'he is in the house', as adjective *-oṛak' gomke* 'house mistress', or as verb - *oṛak'-ked-a-e* 'he made a house', *oṛak'-an-a-e* 'he made a house for himself'.

gOc' straddles the domain of both adjective, i.e. dead- *gOc' hoṛ* 'dead man' *gOc' anḍia* 'dead bullock', and verb i.e. die, kill - *uni gOc'-an-a-e* 'he died', *cẼṛẼ-ko gOc' - ked-e-a* 'they killed the bird'. Similarly, *bapla* is used as noun, i.e. marriage - *baple hoi-en-a* 'the marriage took place', as adjective, i.e. married *bapla hOṛ* 'married person' or as verb i.e. marry-*bapla-en-a-kin* 'they (dl.) were married'.

oka is used as pronoun, i.e. which- *oka-ṭak' do amak'* 'which (thing) is yours' as adverb i.e. where - *oka-calak'-kan'-a-m* 'where are you going' or as verb i.e. to be where - *uni oka-en-a-e* 'where is he gone'.

kuli is used as noun, i.e. question - *amak' kuli dOhOy-mE* 'put your question' and as verb, i.e. to ask - *kuli-ket'-kin-a-e* 'he asked them'. Similarly, *EnEc'* is a noun i.e. dance - *uni-ak'EnEc'* 'her dance', an adjective, i.e. dancing - *EnEc' kuṛi* 'dancing girl' and verb i.e. to dance *EnEc' kar-a-e* 'she is dancing'.

External derivation :

Various morphological processes like prefixation, infixation and suffixation are employed for this type of derivation. This type of derivation is so named as it is externally manifested by the increase in size of the root morpheme. The various morphological processes employed in this type of derivation result in the formation of noun, adjective, adverb and verb.

Nominal Derivation :

In understanding the Santali nominal derivation without ambiguity, it is necessary to explain at least four terms and to say something of normal processes of derivation.

The four terms in question are primary word base, secondary word base, primary derivative and secondary derivative.

Primary word bases in Santali are coterminous with the minimal word and hence are monosyllabic and dissyllabic.

By the incorporation of one affix primary word bases yield primary derivatives. These welcome prefix, suffix and infix.

Some of the primary derivatives function as secondary word bases, i.e. forms of this structure are at once the result of derivation from primary word bases and are capable of serving as a point of departure for further derivation.

The secondary word bases then, by the incorporation of suffixes, yield secondary derivatives.

Normal processes of derivation show five patterns :[4]

A. wb + pfx : *arsal* 'to light' + /ma-/ = *marsal* 'light'

B. wb + inf : *Ol* 'to write' + / -nv- /=*OnOl* 'piece of writing'

C. wb + sfx : (I) *gOc'* 'to die' + /-ic' / = *gOc'ic'* 'dead one'

: (II) *no* 'this' + /-tE / = *nOtE* 'this side'

D. wb = (wb (P) + sfx + sfx) + sfx : *sāo* 'with' +/tE/ (Sociative marker) + /-n/ = *sārtEn* 'accompanying' +/-ic'/ + *sāotEnic'* 'companion'

E. R + wb + sfx : *dadal* 'engaged in beating' *dal* 'to beat' +/-ic' / = *dadalic'* 'one who is engaged in beating'.

In considering the foregoing sets, note that the sub-class (II) of group C includes the primary derivatives of the primary word bases above them and at the same time, secondary word bases of the secondary derivatives below them. These intermediate forms are a necessary step between the primary word base and the secondary derivative.

With these patterns in view different morphological processes — prefixation, infixation and suffixation employed in nominal derivation are to be discussed. And in course of discussion the patterns will be taken care of.

Pattern A : wb + pfx

This is a rare morphological process in Santali. The only prefix found in Santali noun derivation is /ma-/, which functions syntactically as a nominalizer, converting verbs to nouns. It is very restricted in use and only three verb roots are found which take this prefix for nominalization. In some cases, the derived noun carries the meaning of result, that which is resulted from the action of the verb and in some cases the active agent 'he who performs the action of the verb':

Pattern :

Verb	+ D.[5]	/ma-/	*Noun*
arsal	'to light'	/ma-/	*marsal* 'light'
rak'	'to cry'	/ma-/	*marak'* 'peacock'
cEt' '	to teach' /	ma-/	*macEt'* 'teacher'

Pattern B : wb + inf

It is one of the most productive processes of noun- derivation. A huge number of nouns are derived by the application of various infixes, /-tV[6] -/, /-nV -/, /-mV-/, /-rV-/ and /- pV/.

/-tV-/ is infixed into verb roots and adjectives for nominalization. In the monosyllabic roots the infix /-tV-/ is wedged into the root after the vowel which repeats itself after the infix leaving the main part of the infix, i.e. /t/ intervocalic. In case of the dissyllabic roots, normally, the infix is inserted after the vowel of the first syllable. Sporadically, the vowel of the second syllable repeats after the main part of the infix although the infix occurs after the vowel of the first syllable. In many instances the derived noun has a meaning of result, 'that which results from the action of the verb', somewhere 'the actor of the action'. Examples —

Pattern 1 :

Verb root		+*D./ -tV^r-/*	*Noun*	
bOr	'to fear'	/ tV^r/	*bOtOr*	'fear'
rOK'	'to sew'	/-tV^r/	*rOtOK'*	'seam'
ñum	'to name'	/-tV^r/	*ñutum*	'name'
or	'to draw,pull'	/-tV^r/	*OtOr*	'warp of a web'

Pattern 1 :

Verb root		+*D./ -tV^r-/*	*Noun*	
EhOp'	'to begin'	/-tV^r-/	*EtOhOp'*	'beginning'
qORO	'to help'	/-tV^r-/	*qOtORo'*	'help'
SELECT'	'to give company'	/-tV^r-/	*sEtElEt'*	'accompaniment'
sarEc'	'to exceed'	/-tV^r-/	*satarEc'*	'excess'

sahEt'	'to breath'	/-tV^r-/	*satahEt'*	'breath'
OmOn	'to germinate'	/-tV^r-/	*OtOmOn*	'origin'
daram	'to oppose'	/-tV^r-/	*dataram*	'councilor'

Pattern 2 :

Adjective	+D./-tV^r-/	*Noun*	
jeleñ 'long'	/-tV^r-/	*jeteleñ*	'length'

/-ñV^r-/ is infixed into the verb roots and adjective to derive a noun. The infix /-ñV^r-/ is inserted after the first vowel of the root which repeats itself after the main part of the infix, i.e. /n/ making it intervocalic.

The derived nouns sometimes take the meaning of result, i.e. the action performed by the verb — and sometimes the instrument by which the action is performed. Examples —

Pattern 1 :

Verb root		+D./-nV^r-/	*Noun*	
Ol	'to write'	/-nV^r-/	*OnOl*	'written piece'
jOk'	'to sweep'	/-nV^r-/	*jOnOk'*	'broom'
bak'	'to hook'	/-nV^r-/	*banak'*	'hook'
bEt'	'to giver with palm'	/-nV^r-/	*bEnEt'*	'stopper, lie'
qOn'	'to give to marriage'	/-nV^r-/	*qOnOl*	'bride price'
tOl	'to bind',	/-nV^r-/	*tOnOl*	'knot'
dul	'to pour'	/-nV^r-/	*dunul*	'the junction of two river or streams where water falls'
Ol	'to draw patterns'	/-nV^r-/	*OnOl*	'*stripe*'
rakap'	'to rise, ascend'	/-nV^r-/	*ranakap*	'up, develop-ment'
ORhẼ	'to sing in praise'	/-nV^r-/	*OnORhẼ*	song in 'praise'

ãRgo	'to descend'	/-nV^r-/	*ãnaRgo*	'descent'
jORao	'to join'	/-nV^r-/	*jOnORao*	'joint, link'
acur	'to turn'	/-nV^r-/	*anacur*	'winding'
dapal	'to cover'	/-nV^r-/	*danapal*	'cover'
ataṅ	'to receive'	/-nV^r-/	*anataṅ*	'vessel into which anything to be received
EsEst'	'to hinder, check, cover'	/-nV^r-/	*EnEsEt'*	'stopper, covering'
ETEt'	'to make fence'	/-nV^r-/	*EnETEt'*	'partition, fence'
jOR	'to pair'	/-nV^r-/	*jOnOR*	'joint link'
jOt	'to wipe'	/-nV^r-/	*jOnOt'*	'duster'
OR	'to begin'	/-nV^r-/	*OnOR*	'preface'
laRao	'to move, shake'	/-nV^r-/	*lanaRao*	'movement'
harup'	'to embrace'	/-nV^r-/	*hanarup'*	'embracing'
mucat'	'to finish, end'	/-nV^r-/	*munucɘt*	'end'
bidɘ	'to bid farewell'	/-nV^r-/	*minidɘ*	'parting gift'
sudur	'to fall water *from high*'	/-nV^r-/	*sunudur*	' place of the source of water'
qak'	'to stretch twine, thread'	/-nV^r-/	*qanak'*	'spider's web'
qOk'	'to carry on the shoulder'	/-nV^r-/	*qOnOk'*	'a piece of cloth, thrown over the shoulder down to the breast, worn by women'
qOc'	'to kill'	/-nV^r-/	*qOnOc'*	'killing'

Pattern 2 :

adjective		+D./-nV^r-/	Noun	
Osar	'broad'	/-nV^r-/	*OnOsar*	'breadth'
bar	'two'	/-nV^r-/	*banar*	'both'
pE	'three'	/-nV^r-/	*pEnE*	'all three'
Pon	'four'	/-nV^r-/	*ponon*	'all four'

Some verb roots take the infix /-mV^r-/ for nominalisation. The infix is wedged into the root after the first vowel which recurs after the main part of the infix, i.e. /m/. Some also take this infix to derive a further noun denoting specific relation. Examples—

lak'	'to peal, scrap'	/-mV^r-/	*lamak'*	
cEt'	'to teach'	/-mV^r-/	*cEmEt'*	'teaching material'
SElEt'	'to associate'	/-mV^r-/	*SEmlEt'*	'association through *'SEmElet'*

Pattern 2 :

Noun		*D./-mV^r-/*	*Noun*	
hOn	'son'	/-mV^r-/	*hOmOn*	'brother's offspring' (when the Ego is female)

A few verbroots take the infix /-RV^r-/ which is inserted after the first vowel, where V is the vowel of the root itself, so that the main part /R/ becomes intervocal. Examples[3]

Pattern 1 :

Verb root		D./-RV^r-/	*Noun*	
gOm	'to name'	/-RV^r-/	*gOROm*	'grand, namesake'
cẼ	'to squeak'	/-RV^r-/	*cẼRẼ*	'bird'

Pattern 2 :

Noun		*D./-pV^r-/*	*Noun*	
hOn	'child'	/-pV^r-/	*hOpOn*	'children'
manjhi	'village headman'	/-pV^r-/	*mapañji*	'village chiefs'
raj	'king'	/-pV^r-/	*rapaj*	'kind and his retinue'
kisār	'Zamindar'	/-pV^r-/	*kipisə̃r*	'Zamindar and his retinue'
haRam	'old man'	/-pV^r-/	*hapRam*	'ancestor; through hapaRam.

Pattern C : wb + sfx

Like infixation, suffixation plays an important role in noun derivation. Agentive, material, instrumental and locational noun are derived with the suffix /-ic'/ (agentive) /-ak'/ (material). /tEak'/ (instrumental). /-DE/ (locational) and /-tE/ (directional).

Sub - class I :

/-ic'/ is suffixed to the verb roots, verb stems and to adjectives, both primary and derived, to derive a noun denoting a person with that action or quality. Examples —

Pattern 1 :

Verb root/stem		*D/-ic'*	*Noun*	
qOc'	'to die'	/-ic'/	*gOc'ic'*	'dead one'
Ol	'to write'	/- ic'/	*Olic'*	'writer'
EnEc'	'to	/- ic'/	*EnEc'ic'*	'dancer'
KiRiñ	'to buy'	/- ic'/	*kiRiñic'*	'buyer'
əkhriñ	'to sell'	/- ic'/	əkhriñic	'seller'
dadal	'write on and on'	/- ic'/	*dadalic'*	'one who is in the habit of beating'

Pattern 2 :

Adjective (Primary & derived)		*+ D./ic'*	*Noun*	
ponD/põr	'write'	/- ic'/	*ponDic'* / *põRic'*	'write one'
hEndE	'black'	/- ic'/	*hEndEic'*	'black one'
arak'	'red'	/- ic'/	*arak'ic*	'red one'
ETak'	'another'	/- ic'/	*ETak'ic'*	'another one'
boge	'good'	/- ic'/	*bogeic'*	'good one'

In case of the first pattern where the nouns are derived from the verb, action is demanded on the part of the agent. In the second pattern where the nouns are derived from the adjective, primary, derived or phrasal, the derivative form indicates one with a quality, belonging to a place or accompaniment.

/- ak'/ is suffixed to the verbroots and adjectives, primary, derivative and phrasal to derive nouns denoting things with an action or quality. Examples -

Pattern 1 :

Verb root		+ D./-ak'/	*Noun*	
jOm	'to eat'	/- ak'/	*jOmak'*	'food'
Ol	'to write'	/- ak'/	*Olak'*	'written piece'
rOhOy	'to sow'	/- ak'/	*rOhOyak'*	'that which is sown'
kiriñ	'to buy'	/- ak'/	*kiriñak'*	'that which is bought'
akhriñ	'to sell'	/- ak'/	*əkhriñak'*	'that which is sold'

Pattern 2 :

Adjective		+ D./-ak'/	*Noun*	
ponD/põR	'write'	/- ak'/	*ponDak'/'poRak*	'white thing'
hEndE	'black'	/- ak'/	*hEndEak'*	'black thing'
arak'	'red'	/- ak'/	*arakak'*	'red thing'
boge	'good'	/- ak'/	*bogeak'*	'good thing'
ETak'	'another'	/- ak'/	*ETak'ak*	'another thing'
adOm	'some'	/- ak'/	*adOmak'*	'something'

/-tEak'/ is suffixed to a restricted number of verb roots and verb stems to derive nouns denoting instruments that which is used to perform the action of the verb. The composition of /- tEak'/ is by suffixing the derivational suffix /- ak'/ to the instrumental suffix /- tE / Examples —

Pattern :

Demonstrative roots		+ D./-DE/	*Noun*	
no	'this'	/- DE /	*nOnḌE*	'this place'
on	'that'	/-DE /	*OnDE*	'that place'
han	'that yonder'	/-DE /	*hanDE*	'that place yonder'

/-ka/ is suffixed to the simple demonstrative roots *no* 'this' *on* 'that' and *han* 'that yonder' to derive a noun denoting manner. Examples —

Pattern :

Demonstrative root		+ D./-ka/	*Noun*	
no	'this'	/-ka /	*nonka*	'this way'
on	'that'	/-ka /	*onka*	'that way'
han	'that far'	/-ka /	*hanka*	'that way'

Pattern D : *wb (wb(p) + sfx + sfx) + sfx*

The sub-class II of pattern C provides the base as a point of departure for further derivation. The result is secondary derivation from secondary word bases which are in turn the primary derivatives. In considering this sub-class note that the second suffix has the adjectival value and the base is functionally adjectival in nature. Examples –

Pattern :

Adjective (derived)		+ D./-ic'/&/-ak'/	Noun	
sãotEn	'accompanying'	/-ic'/	*sãotEnic*	'companion'
noṅkan	'like this'	/-ic'/	*noṅkanic'*	'one like this'
nOnḌEn	'belonging to this place'	/-ic'/	*nOnDEnic'*	'one belonging to this place
nOtEn	'belonging to this side'	/-ic'/	*nOtEnic'*	'one belonging to this side'
nui lekan	'like this person'	/-ic'/	*nui lekanic'*	'one like this person'
iñrEn	'my'	/-ic'/	*iñrEnic'*	'my one'
noṅkan	'like this'	/-ak'/	*noṅkanak'*	'thing like this'
ondEn	'belonging to that place'	/-ak'/	*OndEnak'*	'thing belonging to that place'
OntEn	'belonging to that side'	/-ak'/	*OntEnak'*	'thing belonging to that side'
buru lekan	'like mountain'	/-ak'/	*buru lekanak'*	'Some thing like mountain'

Pattern : *E : R + wb (p) + sfx*

This pattern is confined to the monosyllabic roots and the suffixes involved are /-ic'/ (animate) and /-ak'/ (inanimate)— The reduplicated word base is functionally adjectival.

Pattern :

Adjective		+ /-ic'/ & /-ak'/	Noun	
dadal	'striking dal to strike'	/-ic'/	*dadalic*	'one who is striking'
gOgOc'	'killing to kill'	/-ic'/	*gogOc'ic'*	'killer'
dadal	'striking'	/-ak'/	*dadalak'*	'striking thing'

Derivation of Adjective :

Adjectives are derived from the simple and derived nouns, derived adverbs, adverbs with locational suffixes, indefinite demonstrative roots, numeral adjectives and *leka*-phrases with the addition of infixes and suffixes. The infixes and suffixes employed in adjective derivation are three in number, one infix and two suffixes.

a. Infixation :

/-nV^r-/ is infixed in the three cardinal numerals only, viz. *bar* 'two' *pE* 'three' and *pon* 'four' to derive inclusive numerals. Here V^r of the infix stands for the vowel of the root.

Pattern :

Cardinal numeral		+ D./-nV^r-/	*Inclusive numeral*	
bar	'two'	/-nV^r-/	*banar*	'both'
pE	'three'	/-nV^r-/	*pEnE*	'all three'
pon	'four'	/-nV^r-/	*ponon*	'all four'

Bodding[7] has accepted these inclusive numerals as nouns without giving any explanation or example whatsoever. Here these derived numerals are treated as both noun and adjective, thus entering into the noun and adjective derivation. As they are used as noun they are also used as attributes in an endocantic attributive construction. Examples —

As adjective		*As noun*	
banar koRa	'both boys'	*bunarge TuTi-kin-mE*	'pierce the both (animals).'
pEnE hORko	'all three men'		
ponon kÕR	'all four corners'	*ponon-ko hEc'-akan-a*	'all four have come'

b. suffixation :

(i) /-an / is suffixed to some primary and derived nouns to derive adjectives denoting possession or quality.

Pattern :

Noun (Simple & derived)		+ *D/- an/*	*Adjective*	
dare	'strength'	/-an /	*darean*	'strong, efficient'
kaDa	'buffalo'	/-an /	*kaDavan*	'one having buffalo'
daya	'kindness'	/-an /	*dayavan*	'kind'

bOtOr	'fear'	/-an /	*bOtOran*	'fearful'
edre	'anger'	/-an /	*edrean*	'angry'

(ii) /-n / is suffixed to derived nouns, derived adverbs, adverbs with directional suffixes, indefinite demonstrative roots (only one) and *leka*-phrases to derive adjectives denoting apputlenance, similarity etc.

Pattern 1 :

Derived noun		*D./-n/*	*Adjective*	
nOnDE	'this place'	/-n /	*nOnDEn*	'belonging to this place (near)'
hanDE	'that place far'	/-n /	*hanDEn*	'belonging to that place (far)'
nOtE	'this side'	/-n /	*nOtEn*	'belonging to this side'
OntE	'that side'	/-n /	*OntEn*	'belonging to that side'
hantE	'that side far'	/-n /	*hantEn*	'belonging to that side (yonder)'.

Pattern 2 :

Derived adverb		*+ D./-n/*	*Adjective*	
nonka	'this'	/-n /	*nonkan*	'like this'
onka	'thus'	/-n /	*onkan*	'like that'
hanka	'that way'	/-n /	*hankan*	'like that'

Pattern 3 :

Adverb + locative		*D./-n/*	*Adjective*	
nui leka	'like this person'	/-n /	*nui lakan*	'id'
uni leka	'like that person'	/-n /	*uni lekan*	'id'
noa leka	'like this thing'	/-n /	*noa lekan*	'id'
oka leka	'like which'	/-n /	*oka lekan*	'id'
jãhã leka	'like anything'	/-n /	*jãhã lekan*	'id'

Derivation of Adverbs : Suffixation is the only process for this derivation and by suffixing /-ka/ to the simple demonstrative root and to the interrogative inanimate demonstrative root a set of manner adverbs is derived.

Pattern 1 :

Simple demonstrative root		*+ D./-ka/*	*Adverb*	
no	'this'	/-ka /	*noṅka*	'thus, in this manner'
on	'that'	/-ka /	*onka*	'thus, in that manner'
han	'that yonder'	/-ka /	*hanka*	'thus, in that manner'
ne	'just this' (N.S.)	/-ka /	*neṅka*	'thus, just in this way'
ni	'id' (S.S)	/-ka /	*niṅkə*	'id'

Pattern 2 :

Interogative demonstrative root		*+ D./-ka/*	*Adverb*	
cet'	'what'	/-ka /	*ceka*	'in what way, how'
cit'	'id'	/-ka /	*cika*	'id'

Derivation of verb roots :

A few verb roots are found to be derived from noun and verb roots by the process of infixation and the infixes /-tV^r-/ and /-nV^r-/ are employed for this purpose.

Pattern 1 :

Noun	*+ D./-tV^r-/*		*Verb*
Or 'foundation'	/-tV^r-/	*otor*	'demolish'

Pattern 2 :

Verb root	*+ D./-nV^r-/*		*Verb*
um 'to wash'	/-nV^r-/	*unum*	'submerge'

Morphophonemic Changes :

The roots and different grammatical morphomes when entered into the morphological processes described above in forming different grammatical classes may change in their phonological shape. It may be assumed that the change in their phonological shape are not so complex as would render them unidentifiable. Different phonological processes employed at the time of combination between the root and the affixes are the following :

(i) Introduction of a vowel glide.

[v] is inserted between a-a, thus

kaDa	+ /-an/	= *kaDavan*
daya	+ /-an/	= *dayavan*

(ii) Elision

a. When two morphemes close, Santali may lose one of the vowels if the preceding morpheme ends and the following morpheme begins with /a/ thus

/ma-/	+ *arsal*	= *marsal*

b. The unstressed vowel may be elided but not as a rule[8]; thus *sElEt'* + /-mV^{r}-/ = *sEmlEt'* instead of expected * *sEmElEt'*

c. t' of *cet'* is elided while /-ka/ is suffixed to it ; thus

cet' + /-ka/ = *ceka.*

(iii) Consonant increment

Before the suffixes /-oE/ and /-ka/ the simple demonstrative root for the proximal *no* gets a nasal increment in analogy with the roots *on* and *han*; thus —

no + /-DE/	= *nOnDE*
no + /-ka/	= *noṅka'*

(iv) Assimilation : The nasal before the stop consonants become homorganic ; thus —

nOnDe = nOṇDE

nonka = noṅka

(v) o of *no* and *on* becomes open when it preceds E, thus -

no + /-DE/ = *nOnDE*

on + /-DE/ = *OnDE*

The foregoing analysis suggests certain points which are important both from synchronic and diachronic perspectives, and also from comparative perspective. The prefixal derivation which is so prevalent in other Austroasiatic languages, particularly Khasi[9] is restricted to only one prefix in Santali. The infixes are numerous, so also the suffixes. The meaning of the affixes are not constant. This is particularly so for the prefix and infixes. The infixes often shuttle between actor and inactive agents and instruments. This polysemic feature is surely a constrain on defining the meaning of the affixes. The question of which meaning is primary and which is secondary may be had from a diachronic angle, but paucity of data is an obstacle at this point. Whether this develops from grammatical changes in the historical languages, can only be explained from a comparative perspective. Because such variations are also found in other non- Munda Austroasiatic languages, particularly in the case of the infixes.[10]

References

1. P.H. Mathews, Morphology. Cambridge : Cambridge University Press. 1974, p. 38.
2. Ibid, p. 43.
3. Richard Hudson, Word Grammar. New York : Basil Blackwell. 1986, p. 73.
4. Wb - Word base, pfx - prefix, inf - infix, sfx - suffix, p - primary and R.-reduplicated.
5. D. stands for derivative.
6. V^r stands for root vowel.'
7. P.O. Bodding, Materials for a Santali Grammar II. Dumka : 1929, p. 46.
8. It may be noted that, in Santali, the first syllable bears the stress. The retention of the unstressed vowel is not uncommon; thus —
   sElEt' + /-tV^r-/ = *sEtElEt'*
   sarEc' + /-tV^r-/ = *satarEc'*
9. K.S. Nagaraja, Khasi : A Descriptive Analysis. Pune : Deccan College, 1985, pp. 9-10.
10. T. Pogibenko, 'Towards the reconstruction of the meaning of two Austroasiatic infixes -m- and -n-', In : M.S. Andronov and B.P. Mallick (eds.), Linguistics : A Soviet Approach. Calcutta : Indian Journal of Linguistics, 1988, pp.262-71.

3

DECLINABLE MORPHEMES

The morphological classes in Santali are primarily based on whether or not they are able to take case affixes and postpositions and show verbal agreement on the basis of animateness or in-animateness. The morphemes which are able to take case markers and which show agreement in the verb are classed under declinables. They are *nominals* with sub-categories nouns and pronouns.

Nominal

Nouns and pronouns are grouped under the same class as they have the the same functional yield in the structure of the language and the former has the same privilege of being used with the suffixes and postpositions as the latter. The major difference between the two is that while on the paradigmatic axis nouns show opposition in number (± gender) and case, the pronouns show opposition in person, number and case.

Noun

Nouns are divided into primary, consisting of roots only and secondary or derived nouns. The formation of the secondary or derived nouns are discussed in the chapter of derivation in detail. So, here the noun derivation with its various employs is not taken up for consideration. The nouns are capable of showing opposition in number and case and a few of them also show opposition in gender. But gender is not a grammatical category in Santali, as it doesn't have any impact on the structure of the language, i.e. it is not functional. Moreover, the morphemes which show opposition in gender are borrowings from either Hindi or Bengali and the native nouns which are affected by this process are the results of analogical extension. Examples —

koRa 'boy / young man'

koRakin 'two boys / young man'

koRako 'boys / young men'

koRarEn 'of the boy / young man' (animate)

koRakorEn 'of the boys / young men' (animate)

koRakoak' 'of the boys / young men' (inanimate)

kuRi '*girl* / young lady'

kuRikin 'two girls / young ladies'

kuRikinak' 'of the two girls / young ladies' (inanimate)

kuRikinrEn 'of the two girls / young ladies' (animate)

əndiə pusi 'male cat'

əndiə pusikin 'two male cats'

eṅga pusi 'female cat'

eṅga pusiko 'female cats'

gəDi 'car'

gəDiko 'cars'

gəDikorE 'in the cars'

From the examples cited, the grammatical construction of Santali nouns may be shown as below :

N = Root (± gender) + / number + / - case

Classification of nouns

The nouns can be classified both on the paradigmatic axis and the syntagmatic axis. In both the axis, different factors are involved in the classification of nouns :

I. Classification on paradigmatic axis

(i) On the paradigmatic axis depending on whether or not the noun is derived by employing the suffixes /-ic' / and /-ak' / the nouns can be sub-grouped into two classes, viz., a. the nouns denoting animate beings ; and b. the nouns that refer to inanimate objects. Example —

a.	*rOhOyic'*	'sower'
	ponDic'	'the white one'
	hEndEic'	'the black one'
	arak'ic'	'the red one'
b.	*Olak'*	'that which is written'
	rOhOyak'	'that which is sown'
	ponDak'	'the white thing'
	jOmak'	'food'

(ii) Again, depending on whether or not the nouns can be substituted by *uni* 'he, that person' the nouns can be classified into two classes, viz.,

a. the nouns that refer to animate human beings; and

b. the nouns that refer to animate non-human beings.

Example —

birsa calak'-kan-a-e	'Diran is going'
uni calak'-kan-a-e	'he is going'
phulmoni calak'-kan-a-e	'Phulmani is going'
uni calak'-kan-a-e	'she is going'
seta gEgEr-kan-a-e	'the dog is biting'

but not *uni gEgEr-Kan-a-e.*

(iii) Depending on whether or not the nouns take the locative suffixes /-rE/ or /-tE/ the nouns can be sub-grouped under two categories, viz.,

a. the nouns that refer to animate beings ;

b. the nouns that refer to inanimate objects;

i.e. animate nouns cannot take the suffixes cited above while inanimate nouns are capable of taking them;

Example —

kharańrE	'in the hole'
dak'rE	'in the water'
birrE	'in the forest'
birtE	'to the forest'
iskultE	'to the school'
ñutrE	'in the dark'

II. Classification of nouns on syntagmatic axis

(i) Depending on whether or not the nouns are incorporated in the verb as subject or object in the form of the personal clitic pronouns the same two-way classification holds, viz.,

a. the nouns referring to animate beings;

b. the nouns referring to inanimate objects; i.e. the animate nouns are incorporated in the verb while the inanimate nouns are not ; Example —

birsə gOc' - en-e-(e)	'Birsa died'
phulmoni jOk'-ed-a-(e)	'Phulmoni is sweeping'
seta dOn-ed-a-(e)	'the dog is jumping'
sukcãd cẼRẼ gOc'-ked-(e)-a- (e)	'Sukchani killed the bird'
but not *dare ultə-en-a-(e)*	'the tree fell'
instead *dare ultau-en-a*	'the tree fell'

(ii) Again, depending on whether the governed noun is animate or inanimate the genitive case affixes and postpositions are chosen. The suffixes /-ic'/ and /-rEn/ are used with the possessor noun or pronoun provided the governed noun is animate and the suffixes /-ak'/, /-ań/, /-rEak'/, /-rEań /, rEanak'/ and

/-rEnaṅ/ are chosen, provided the noun possessed is inanimate; Example —

birsərEn hOpOn	'Birsa's son'
iñic' gəi or *iñrEn* gəi	'my cow'
amic' mErOm	'thy goat'
amak' katha	'thy word'
darerEak' jO	'the fruit of the tree'
darerEṅak' jO	'id'
birrEnaṅ dare	'the tree of the forest'
amaṅ ti	'thy hand'
lOkhOnak' oRak'	'Lakhan's house'

From the above discussions the following tabular form can be formulated to posit the classification of noun —

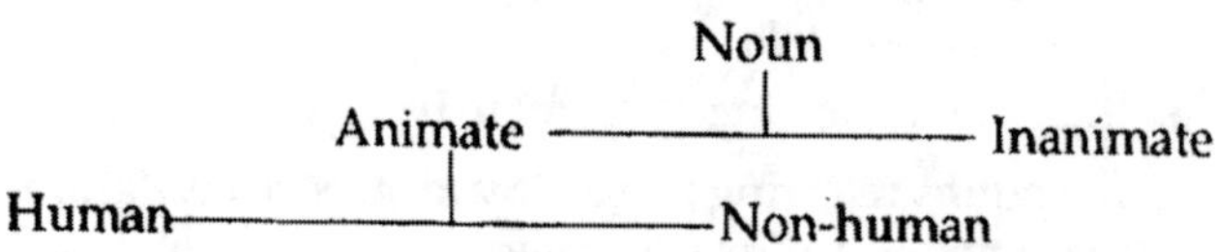

Though the nouns are broadly classified as animates and inanimates, some further comments should be made about animate nouns as they cover a wide range of concepts. Besides the living beings, the following objects are also considered animate.

(i) The celestcal bodies, i.e. the sun, the moon and the stars are animate ; Example —

siñcādo rakap'-kan-a- (e)	'the sun is rising'
ñindacādo Dubuc'-en-a- (e)	'the moon set'
holarEn ipil-iñ ñEl-ket'-(ko)-a	'I saw the stars of yesterday'

(ii) Spiritual beings and spirits are regarded as animate ; Example—

uni mit 'Taṅ kaliboṅga benao-akad-(e)-a-(e)	'he has made a Kali idol'
uni bongo-e bOtOr - (ako)-a	'he is afraid of the ghosts'

(iii) Puff-ball, ear-wax, the complete shells of the snails, thorn when pricked are regarded as animate ; Example —

puTka-ko halañ-ket'-(ko)-a 'they collected mushrooms'

ẼrgOt' menak'-(kO)-a- 'there are ear-waxes'

iñ iñrEn jhinuk-iñ rapak'- ket'-(ko)-a 'I burnt my shells'

jənum-iñ tot'-ked-(e)-a 'I extracted the thorn'

(iv) Any painting or idol representing a living being is considered animate; Example -

unirEn pEa putul menak'-(ko)-a 'he/she has three dolls'

onko / unku kãtrE janwar-ko benao-akat'-(ko)-a 'they have drawn animals on the wall'

(v) The dead human beings and animals are regarded as animate provided the name is used or the person is referred to; Example —

gOc' hOR-ko agu-ked-(e)-a 'they brought the dead man'

iñrEn gOc' hOR 'my dead man'

unirEn gOc' ənDia 'his dead ox'

The nominative, accusative are left unmarked as there are no overt case markers for them. There are overt case markers for the instrumental, dative, ablative, genitive and locative. The case markers occured with the sub-groups of nouns which are tabulated below.

		Animate	Inanimate
Instrumental	case marker	-tE	-tE
Dative	case marker	a-	---
Ablative	case marker	khOn, Kh Onak', KhOnan (S.S) KhOx' (N.S)	khOnak', khOnañ(S.S) khOc' (N.S.)
Genitive	case marker	t-, -ic' (Sg.) -rEn (pl) (S.S.) -rEn (N.S.)	-añ, rEañ, -rEnak' - rEnañ (S.S.) -ak' - rEak' (N.S.)
Locative (rest)	case marker		-rE
Locative (motion)	case marker		-tE

Examples —

	Animate	Inanimate
Instrumental:	*iñ(tE)ge-ñ mak' - akan- a* 'I am cut by myself'	*Dan (tE) tiyok '-mE '* pull down with the stick'
Dative:	*gOrO-(añ)*-mE 'help me'	---------
Ablative:	*gidrə-(khOn) hatao-mE(S.S.)* *gidra-(khOc') hatao-mE (N.S.)* 'take (it) from the child'	*dak'-(khOn) rakap'hijuk'-kan-a-e* 'he is coming up from the water' *dare-(khOnak') ul ñurhak'-kan-a* 'mango is falling from the tree' *dare-(khoc') ãRgon-mE* 'get down from the tree' (N.S.)
Genitive:	*lOkhonn-(ic') gidra* 'Lakhan' son' (Sg.)	*am- (an) katha* 'thy word' *dare-(rEnak') jo'* 'fruit of the tree'
	hOR-(rEn) gidra 'children of the man' (Pl)	*iñ-(ak') ti* 'My hand'
	OtOr-(rEak') sutəm	'string of the wrap' (N.S.)
	ato-(rEn) mañjhi 'headman of the village'	N.S.
	pon hOR- (rEn) ponea gidrə *'four children of four men'*	
Locative : Rest		*'kami-(rE)* in action'
Motion		*iskul-(tE) calak'- mE* 'go to school'

Pronoun

The pronouns in Santali show opposition in person, number and case and some also show opposition is being animate and inanimate on the paradigmatic axis, and on the syntagmatic axis fill the slot of noun. Unlike noun, the personal pronouns have separate lexical identities for different persons and numbers except in the third person where dual and plural are derived from the same root as in the singular by adding the respective number suffixes. The demonstrative pronouns, show variation for the animate and the inanimate, for what is definite and what is in-definite. Some of the interrogative pronouns are derived from the interrogative pronouns themselves, with the addition of certain particles and some are echo formations.

Pronouns, as already noted, are capable of showing opposition in person, number and case, for instance—

iñ 'I'	*alañ* 'we (two) (incl.)'	*abo* 'we (incl.)'
uni 'he'	*unkin* 'they (two)'	*onko/unku* 'they'
unitE 'by him'	*unkin-tE* 'by them(two)'	*onko-tE/unku- tE'* 'by then
unirEn 'of him'	*unkin-rEn* 'of them (two)'	*onko-rEn/unku-rEn* 'of them
OkOe 'who'	*OkOekin* '*who* (two)'	*OkOeko* (who) (all)'

From the examples cited above the grammatical construction of a pronoun can be formulated thus :

Pronoun = Root + Person + Number+/- case.

The demonstrative pronouns again show opposition in being animate or inanimate. For example —

Simple Demonstrative :	*nui* 'this 'one'	*noa* 'this (thing)'
Interrogative Demonstrative:	*OkOe* 'who'	*oka* 'which'
Indefinite Demonstrative :	*jāhāe* 'anyone'	*jāhā* 'anything'

Pronouns, in Santali, can be classified into personal and demonstrative. Of these, the personal pronouns are representated by separate lexical items except in the third person which, actually a distal demonstrative for animate, forms its dual and plural with the addition of the dual and plural suffixes /-kin/ and /-ko/ respectively, to the distal demonstrative root *on* 'that'. The demonstratives have separate forms for the animate and inanimate which are, in turn, derived from common roots.

Besides these, there is another pronoun, viz., reflexive, represented by only one lexical item, the dual and plural being formed by adding the respective number suffixes, but that is confined to third person only. The reason for considering that form of pronoun is that it is used as the third personal pronoun as well.

Personal Pronoun

The personal pronouns in Santali have separate forms for the three persons, three numbers- singular, dual and plural, along with separate forms for the inclusive i.e. including the person addressed and exclusive i.e. excluding the same, in the first person dual and plural. The personal pronouns do not show gender sex distinction. The same form is used for both masculine and feminine.

The personal pronouns are used either independently or in suffixed or infixed forms. The independent forms of the personal pronouns available in my data are as follows :

		Singular	Dual	Plural
Ist person	Incl.	iñ	alaṅ	abo
	Excl.		aliñ	alE
2nd person		am	aben/abin	apE
3rd person		uni	unkin	onko/unku

The third personal pronoun *uni* 'he' is derived from the distal demonstrative root *on* 'that' with the animate suffix /-i/. In the Southern dialect the root after morphophonemic change is taken as the stem for the dual and plural i.e. the dual and plural suffixes /-kin/ and /-ko/ respectively are added to it. In the Northern dialect, on the other hand, the root *on* remains intact in the plural i.e. *onko.*

All these independent forms of the personal pronouns can fill the subject slot of a sentence. And like noun, they take all case affixes and postpositions except the locative, e.g.

iñ jOk'-ed-añ	'I am sweeping'
iñtE	'by me'
iñkhon	'from me'
iñrEn	'of me' (animate)
iñak'	'of me' (inanimate)
iñihEn	'near me'
iñsão	'with me'
iñlǝgit'	'for me'

The personal pronominal forms incorporated in the verb phrase to refer to the person and number of the subject are tabulated below:

		Singular	Dual	Plural
Ist person	Inclusive	iñ – -ñ	-laṅ	-bon/-bo
	Exclusive		-liñ	-lE
2nd person		-m -em -mE	-ben / -bin	-pE
3rd person		-e	-kin	-ko

The bound morphs of the personal pronouns tabulated above have different functions. Basically, they are incorporated in the verb phrase i.e. either suffixed to the verb at the end or to the word preceding it, to mark the subject. Excepting the third person, they are also used to indicate the possessor pronoun.

As Subject Markers

The incorporation of the animate subject in the form of bound morphs of the personal pronouns in the verb or the word immediately preceding is obligatory in Santali. When an animate noun fills the slot of the subject in a sentence, it is incorporated in the verb phrase in the bound forms of the third personal pronoun, the choice of singular, dual or plural depending on the number of the subject. When a personal pronoun functions, as the subject in a sentence, it is marked in the verb phrase in its bound form. The distribution of the different allomorphs is a follows :

a. /iñ~ - ñ / : The condition in which one or the other occurs is purely phonological, i.e. / iñ/ occurs after words ending in a consonant and /-ñ/ occurs after words ending in a vowel ; e.g.

iñ Takalagit'-(iñ) calak'-kan-a 'I am going for money'
iñ hola-(ñ) sEn-len-a OR iñ hola sEn-len-a-(ñ) 'I went yesterday'
iñ jOm-ed-a(ñ) OR iñ- (iñ) jOm-ed-a 'I am eating'

b. /S-m̃-em, -mE/ : The occurrence of the first two allomorphs depends on phonological conditions, i.e. /-m/ occurs after words ending in a vowel and after consonants it becomes /-em/

am daka-(m) jOm-a? Will you eat rice ?' OR 'Do you eat rice ?'

am iskul-(em) calao-en-a ? 'Did you go to the school ?'

The occurrence of the allomorph /-mE / is morphologically conditioned i.e. it is used in the imperative mood only ; e.g.

calak'-mE 'go'

jOm-mE 'Eat'

c. All other allomorphs are the cliptic forms of the independent personal pronouns without the initial /a-/. The allomorphs of the third personal dual and plural are the dual and plural number suffixes, the demonstrative root being left out.

Allomorphs are suffixed to kinship terms to indicate the possessor: The allomorphs suffixed to the kinship terms to indicate the possessors are /iñ~-ñ / in the first person, / -m~-mE/ in the second person and /-t~-tEt'/ in this case. Examples are —

hOpOniñ	'my / our son'
bOkOñ	'my / our younger brother'
Eṅgam	'thy / your mother'
kiminmE	'thy / your daughter-in-law'
hilit	'his / this sister-in-law'
kimintEt'	'his / their daughter-in-law'

Along with the subject pronoun the object pronoun is also marked in the verb in an infixed form. The infixed forms of the personal pronouns are tabulated below.

		Singular	Dual	Plural
1st person	Inclusive	-iñ ~ -ñ-	–laṅ–	–bon–
	Exclusive		–liñ–	–iE–
2nd person		-me-	-ben-/-bin-	-pE-
3rd person		-e-	-kin-	-ko-

Example are —

uni iñ-e-dal-ked (iñ)-a	'he beat me'
durup' -oco- (ñ) - kan-a-e	'he is causing me to sit'

gOc' - (me)-a-e	'he will kill you'
dal-(e)-mE	'beat him'
seta dO gEr-kin-a-e	'the dog will bite them two'
ñEl-(ko)-m	'see them'

Demonstrative Pronoun

Demonstrative pronouns unlike nouns and personal pronouns take a restricted number of suffixes and postpositions and take definite articles. Demonstrative pronouns are three – the simple demonstrative, the interrogative demonstrative and the indefinite demonstrative.

Simple Demonstrative

They have different forms according to whether they refer to the animate or to the inanimate. Along with this, different types of demonstratives are found deitically. Again, further demonstrative forms are found which are particularised and intensified besides demonstratives which refer to what is seen and what is heard.

There are five demonstrative roots attested in my data and the different simple demonstratives are formed from this. They are – *no, ne* (N.S.)/*ni* (S.S.), *han, nO* and *Ot*. The first two roots shift their vowels in the initial position in forming the distal demonstratives, thus *on* and *en/in*. *han* forms the base of the remotal demonstrative. *ne/ni* with variants *en/in* forms the base of the particularised demonstrative, *no* forms the base of the proximal demonstrative, *nO* forms the base of the inanimate intensified demonstrative, *Ot* forms the base of the demonstrative referring to what is heard.

Deictic classification of the ordinary simple demonstrative pronouns.

	Animate	Inanimate
Proximal	Sg. *nui* 'this'	*noa* 'id'
	Dl. *nukin* 'these two'	*noakin* 'id'
	Pl. *noko/nuku* 'these'	*noako* 'id'
Distal	Sg. *uni* 'that'	*ona* 'id'
	Dl. *unkin* 'those two'	*onakin* 'id'
	Pl. *onko/unku* 'those'	*onako* 'id'

Remotal	Sg. *hani* 'that yonder'	*hana* 'id'
	Dl. *hankin* 'those two yonder'.	*hanakin* 'id'
	Pl. *hanko* 'those yonder'	*hanako* 'id'

Deictic classification of the particularised demonstrative pronouns derived from the root *ne/ni* with its variant *en/in*.

	Animate	Inanimate
Proximal	Sg. *nii* 'just this '	*nia* 'id'
	Dl. *nikin* 'just these two'	*niakin* 'id'.
	Pl. *neko/niku* 'just these'	*niako* 'id'
Distal	Sg. *ini 'just that'*	*ina* 'id'
	Dl. *inkin* 'just those two'	*inakin* 'id'
	Pl. *enko/inku* 'just those'	*inako* 'id'
Remotal	———	———

Intensified Demonstrative Pronouns

These are formed by infixing /-k'-/ either to the ordinary demonstrative pronoun for the animate *nui* 'this one' or the particularised demonstrative pronoun *nii* 'just this one' or to the demonstrative root *nO* 'this (inanimate)'; thus,

nuk'ui 'this very one' from *nui* 'this one'

nik'i 'this very one' from *nii* 'just this one'

nOk'Oy 'this very thing' from *nO* 'this (inanimate)

The dual and plural of the first two forms are not found, the gap being filled up by the dual and plural of the ordinary demonstrative pronouns *nukin* and *nuku/noko*, and particularised *nikin* and *neko/niku* respectively. *nOk'Oy* take /*kin*/ and /*ko* to form the dual and the plural respectively.

Demonstrative Pronoun refering to sight

Two types of distance are possible in this kind of demonstrative pronouns – distal and remotal, one being formed from the distal counterpart of the root *no* and the other from *han*.

Distal	Remotal
Sg. *OnE* 'that seen there'	*hanE* 'that seen yonder'

OnEkin 'those two seen there'	*hanEkin* 'those two seen yonder'
OnEko 'those seen there'	*hanEko* 'those seen yonder'

Demonstrative Pronouns refering to sound

Only distal form with dual and plural of this type of pronoun is attested in my data.

Sg.	*OtE*	'that thing heard'
Dl.	*OtEkin*	'those two heard'
Pl.	*OtEko*	'those heard'

Interrogative Demonstrative Pronoun

Interrogative pronoun distinguishes between animate and inanimate and the definite and the indefinite. There are two interrogative roots *oko* and *ce* from which the pronouns are formed. The definite interrogative pronoun for the animate is formed by adding /-e/ 'he', short form of the third personal pronoun to *oko* and the inanimate by adding /-a/ to the same. The indefinite interrogative are formed from *ce* where /le/ is added for the animate and /t'/ for the inanimate.

	Animate	Inanimate
Definite	Sg. *OkOe* 'who'	*oka* 'which'
	Dl. *OkOekin* 'who two'	*okakin* 'which two'
	Pl. *OkOeko* 'who all'	*okako* 'which all'
Indefinite	Sg. *cele/cili* 'who what'	'*cet'/cit'*' 'what'
	Dl. *celekin/ cilikin*	*cet'kin / cit'kin*
	Pl. *celeko / ciliko*	*cet'ko / cit'ko*

Indefinite Demonstrative Pronoun

The indefinite demonstrative pronouns also distinguish between the animate and the inanimate. There is only one root *jãhã* 'any' from which the demonstrative pronouns are formed. The animate form is formed by adding /-e/ to *jãhã* and the animate form then forms the base for dual and plural. The root itself functions as inanimate.

	Animate	Inanimate
	Sg. *jãhãe* 'anyone'	*jãhã* 'anything'
	Dl. *jãhãekin* 'any two'	*jãhãkin* 'any two'
	Pl. *jãhãeko* 'any all'	*jãhãko* 'any all'

Addition of personal suffix /-ic'/ and impersonal /-ak'/ to the adjective *ETak'* 'another' and derived adjective *jāhãn* 'any' are also used as indefinite pronouns. *adOm* 'some' is also used as indefinite pronoun for the animate and for the inanimate it takes the impersonal /-ak'/. Thus —

	Animate	Inanimate
Sg.	*ETak 'ic'* 'another one'	*ETak 'ak'* 'another thing'
Dl.	*ETak 'kin'* 'other two'	*ETak' ak 'kin'* 'other two thing'
Pl.	*ETak' ko* 'other ones'	*ETak 'ak' ko* 'other things'
Sg.	*jāhãnic'* 'any one'	*jāhãnak'* 'any thing'
Dl.	*jāhãnkin* 'any two'	*jāhãnak 'kin'* 'any two thing'
Pl.	*jāhãnko* 'any more'	*jāhãnak'ko* 'any things'
Sg.	*adOm* 'some'	*adOmak'* 'something'
Dl.	*adOmkin* 'some two'	*adOmak 'kin'* 'something two'
Pl.	*adOmko* 'some all'	*adOmak' ko* 'something more'

Morphophonemic Changes

The different demonstrative roots when combine with different personal and non-personal suffixes are subject to the following morphophonemic changes :

a. /o/ is realised as[u] when preceded or followed by high front vowel in the same syllable or next ; e.g.

no + i = nui

on + i = uni

in + ko = inko

ni + ko = niku

b. /a/ when preceded or followed by high front vowel it is realised as [ə] ; e.g.

han + – i = hani

ni + – a = niə

in + – a = inə

c. Before the third personal marker /-e/ oko is realised as OkO, as

oko + – e = OkOe

d. Before k the dental checked t' is realised as alveolar checked ṭ' thus

cet' + – kin = ceṭ' kin

cet' + – ko = ceṭ'ko

Number

Number as a grammatical category affects the nominals and the verbs in Santali. There are three numbers — singular, dual and plural. Number, when it affects the verb represents the person and number of the animate subject and/or object. The inanimate subject is left unmarked. The personal pronouns have separate forms for the three numbers in the first and second person. Only the third person, takes dual and plural suffixes to form their dual and plural forms. Normally, the singular number is left unmarked, i.e. the absence of a suffix denotes the singular number. There are separate suffixes for dual and plural.

Singular Number

(i) ϕ (unmarked)

The stem forms of Nominals when unmarked are to be understood as singular number. In case of the verb, the animate subject or object noun or pronoun in the singular number is represented in the verb phrase by using the bound forms of the respective pronouns.

Examples showing the occurrence of singular number —

a. After noun stems :

– *sets*,,	+ /-ϕ/ = *seta*	'dog'
hOR	+ /-ϕ/ = *hOR*	'men'

b. After pronoun stems :

uni	+ /ϕ/ = *uni*	'he'
ona	+ /ϕ/ = *ona*	'that (inanimate)'
OkOe	+ /ϕ/ = *OkOe*	'who'
oka	+ /ϕ/ = *oka*	'which'
jãhã	+ /o/ = *jãhãe*	'anyone'
jãhã	+ /o/ = *jãhã'*	anything'

c. In verb phrase :

seta gEgErkana(e) 'the dog is barking' (subject marked)

uni hOR-(e) gOc'ked(e)a 'he killed the man' (subject and object both marked)

(ii) The derived animate nouns and pronouns with the person suffix /- ic'/ serve to express the singular number. Examples—

dadalic' 'one who beats'

jāhānic' 'any one'

(iii) The dual forms of the first and second personal pronouns are used to express the singular number and this occurs only among the kinship relations.

Parents-in-law and children-in-law when addressing each other use the 2nd person dual and when talking to each other and referring to themselves use the exclusive form of the first person when only one person is meant. Example—

ceka-en-a-ben, bahu 'how are you, daughter-in-law'

ruak'-kan-a-liñ 'I am getting fever'

(iv) Co-parents-in-law in addressing each other and in talking to themselves use the inclusive form of the first person plural when just one person is meant. Example—

hEnda ho, sumdhi, cet'leka menak'-bon-a? 'O, co-parent-in-law, how are you ?'

adi muskilrE-bon paRao-akan-a 'I am in great difficulties'

(v) There is no honorific pronoun as such in Santali. But under the influence of the IA. languages the educated Santals are using the dual form of the second personal pronoun to address and talk to a respected, senior and even to unknown persons.

(vi) There is also a lexical way of expressing the singular number with the help of the numeral *mit'* 'one'. Example —

mit' koRa 'one boy / youngman'

mit' serma 'one year'

Dual Number

(i) The specific suffix for denoting the dual number is /-kin/. This occurs after all nominal stems excepting the 1st and 2nd personal pronouns. It is also shown in the verb to mark the number of animate subject and object. Examples—

a. After noun stems :

hOR	+ /-kin/	= *hORkin*	'two men'
seta	+ /-kin/	= *setakin*	'two dogs'
dare	+ /-kin/	= *darekin*	'two trees'

b. After pronoun stems :

nui	+ /-kin/	= *nukin*	'these two' (animate)
uni	+ /-kin/	= *unkin*	'those two' (animate)
ona	+ /-kin/	= *onakin*	'those two' (inanimate)
OkOe	+ /-kin/	= *OkOekin*	'who two' (animate)
oka	+ /-kin/	= *okakin*	'which two' (inanimate)
jāhāe	+ /-kin/	= *jāhāekin*	'any two' (animate)
jāhā	+ /-kin/	= *jāhākin*	'any two' (inanimate)

c. In a Verb phrase :

unkin rOpORkana(kin) 'they two are quarreling with each other' *dal(kin)mE* 'beat them two' (object marked)

The derived animate nouns and pronouns with the personal suffix /-ic'/ and the animate demonstrative pronouns in /-i/ first dispense with their /-ic'/ and /-i/ and then take the dual suffix /-kin/ to form the dual.

Example —

Singular		Dual	
dadalic'	'one who beats'	*dadalkin*	'two who beat'
OOlic'	'writer'	Olkin	'two writers'
jāhānic	'any one'	*jāhānkin*	'any two'

uni	'he / that person'	*unkin*	'those two persons'
nui	'this person'	*nukin*	'those two persons'
hani	'that person yonder'	*hankin*	'those two persons yonder'

(ii) The lexical way of expressing the dual number with the numeral for two either before or after the object counted, with or without the classifier. Example —

bar hOR	'two men'
barea sim	'two hen'
barea Dańra	'two bullocks'
bar kos	'two kros'
Dańra barea	'two bullocks'

Plural Number

(i) The suffix used after the nominals excepting the first and the second personal pronouns to form the plural is /-ko/. It is also shown in the verb to mark the plural animate subject and object and in that case the plural suffix after the subject nominals may be dispensed with in favour of the same suffix shown in the verb. Example —

a. After noun :

hOR	+ /-ko/	=	*hORko* 'men'
janoar	+ /-ko/	=	*janoarko* 'animals'
hapRam	+ /-ko/	=	*hapRamko* 'ancesters'
TuDu	+ /-ko/	=	*TuDuko* 'Tudu men' (sept)

b. After pronoun :

ona	+ /-ko/	=	*onako* 'those' (inanimate)
noa	+ /-ko/	=	*noako* 'these' (inanimate)
OkOe	+ /-ko/	=	*OkOeko* 'who all' (animate)
oka	+ /-ko/	=	*okako* 'which all (inanimate)
jãhãe	+ /-ko/	=	*Jãhãeko* 'any men'
jãhã	+ /-ko/	=	*jãhãko* 'anything'

c. In verb phrase :

ñEl-let'-(ko)-a-ñ 'I saw them'

hORko calao-en-a-(ko) OR *hOR calao-en-a-(ko)* 'the men went'

(ii) Sometimes, /-ko/ with the addition of /ta-/, hence /tako/, serves as the plural marker. Thus —

TuDu + /-tako/ = *TuDutako* 'Tudu men'

hOpOneañ + /-tako/ = *hOpOnerañtako* 'my daughters'

(iii) Sometimes, numerals higher than 'two' and words indicating plurality are used before the nouns counted to indicate the plural.

ponon hOR	'four men'	*thora hOR*	'some men'
ponon kõR	'four sides'	*adom hOR*	'some men'
pE hOR	'three men'	*dOme dokan*	'so many shop'
ayma din	'many days'	*dOme parkOm*	'So many cots'
ayma hOR	'many men'	*kichu hOR*	'some men'
ayma dokan	'many shops'	*amda hOR*	'many men'
jOto/ jhOtO hOpOnerat	'all daughters'	*amda dokan*	'many shops'
sanam hOR	'all men'	*adhan hOR*	'some men'
sanam TanDi	'the whole field'		

Concerning the category of gender :

The gender is not a grammatical category in Santali as it does not affect the grammatical pattern of the language. It has rather a classificatory bias extending over different sexes and in that case male, female and common gender are classified.

Certain nouns ending in /-a/ replace the sound by /-i/ to form the feminine. Example—

koRa	'boy / young man'	*kuRi*	'girl / young lady'
bheDa	'ram'	*bhiDi*	'sheep'
bhola	'dog'	*bhuli*	'bitch'
mama	'maternal uncle'	*mami*	'maternal aunt'

kala	'deaf'	*kali*	'deaf'
korika	'mad, foolish'	*kuṅki*	'id'
khepa	'mad'	*khipi*	'id'
leṅra	'lame'	*lenri*	'id'
totra	'having a defect in speech'	*tutri*	'id'
koDa	'dumb'	*kuDi*	'id'
phogra	'toothless'	*phugri*	'id'
caDra	'bald headed'	*caDri*	'id'

There is another type of sex distinction purely a lexical one where separate words for male and female are used. Example —

Masculine		Feminine	
əndiə	'ox'	*gəi*	'cow'
bOyha	'brother'	*misEra*	'sister'
jãvãy	'husband'	*bəhu*	'wife'
ba	'father'	*yu*	'mother'
hErEl	'man,husband'	*mayjiu*	'woman, wife'
apat	'father'	*eṅgat*	'mother'
kaDa	'buffalo'	*bitkil*	'do fem.'
haRam	'grand father, old man'	*buRhi*	'grand mother, old woman'
bəbu	'little boy'	*məi*	'little girl'

Sex is sometimes indicated by using words for male and female before or after a word indicating common noun. Example—

Masculine		Feminine	
ənDiə pusi	'cat'	*eṅga pusi*	'do fem.'
ənDiə sadOm	'horse'	*eṅga sadOm*	'mare'
ənDiə mihu	'male calf'	*eṅga mihũ*	'fem. calf'
ənDiə seta	'dog'	*eṅga seta*	'bitch'

ənDiə sukri	'male pig'	*eṅga sukri*	'fem. pig'
ənDiə gEDe	'male duck'	*eṅga gEDe*	'fem. duck'
ənDiə miru	'male parrot'	*eṅga miru*	'fem. parrot'
ənDiə potam	'male dove'	*eṅga potam*	'fem. dove'
sanDi sim	'cock'	*eṅga sim*	'hen'
sanDi paora	'male pigeon'	*eṅga paora*	'fem. pigeon'
pẼThar mihũ	'male calf'	*bachi mihũ*	'fem. calf'
koRa gidrə	'boy'	*kuri gidrə*	'girl'
koRa hOpOn	'son'	*kuRi hOpOn*	'daughter'
kuDu sukri OR sukri kuDu	'boar'	*paThi sukri*	'she- pig, sow'
gOROm kora	'grand son'	*gOROm kuRi*	'grand daughter'
hOñhariñ haRam	'male co-parent -in-law'	*hOñhariñ buRhi*	'fem., co-parent-in-law'
saṅgat koRa	'boy friend'	*saṅgat kuRi*	'girl friend'

Morphophonemic changes

The masculine forms in /-a/ when replace it by /-i/ in forming their feminine counterparts enter into the following morphophonological changes—

Vowel harmony :

(i) /o/ and /e/ preceding /i/ in the very next syllable are pronounced as [u] and [i] respectively ; e.g.

koRa	+	/-i/	=	kuRi
bhola	+	/-i/	=	bhuli
koṅka	+	/-i/	=	kuṅki
totra	+	/-i/	=	tutri
koDa	+	/-i/	=	kuDi

phogra	+	/-i/	=	phugri
bheDa	+	/-i/	=	bhiDi
lenra	+	/-i/	=	linri

(ii) /a/ preceding /i/ in the very next syllable is pronounced as [ə]; e.g.

kala	+	/-i/	=	kali
mama	+	/-i/	=	mami
cəDra	+	/-i/	=	cəDri

Case :

Case, in Santali, is effected by the use of affixes (prefix and suffixes) and postpositions. The declension as seen in the inflexional languages is absent. Instead, the suffixes and postpositions are used after the stem to denote different cases without affecting the phonetic shape of the stem. The case affixes and postpositions occur after both primary and secondary nouns and pronouns with the exception that some occur after the animate and some after the inanimate. They are added to the nouns and pronouns or to the number affixes and enclitic definitives added to them. In certain cases, as in the locative, the use of the case markers is restricted to the animate or to the inanimate. Again, in certain cases as in the genitive, there is a sharp distinction in the selection of the case affixes and postpositions i.e. one set of the affixes and postpositions for the animate and another for the inanimate. No affixes and postpositions occurs in the nominative and the accusative. In certain cases, as in the ablative and the genitive, compound case markers occur. The dialectal differences in the choice of case affixes and postpositions are also noticed as in the southern dialect in the genitive, a sharp distinction between the, singular and the plural has been curiously developed. As the nouns and pronouns behave alike in case, both are to be dealt with together.

Santali substantives can be said to have eight cases : Nominative, Accusative, Instrumental, Dative, Ablative, Genitive, Locative and Sociative. S. Bhattacharya in discussing the case system in the Munda languages, has mentioned seven cases without mentioning the sociative under separate heading. He has incorporated the sociative within the instrumental. But as there are separate postpositions to mark this case relation it is better to posit a separate case rather then incorporating it into another.

I. **Nominative:** (ϕ) There is no separate affix or postposition to mark the nominative. It is, instead, marked in the verb phrase, either at the end of the verb or the word immediately preceding it in the bound forms of the personal pronouns. The noun if it is animate is marked in the verb phrase in the bound forms of the third personal pronoun, singular or non-singular. If a personal pronoun is in the nominative it is marked by its shortened form. The inanimate noun and pronoun are not marked in the verb. Example —

uni ñEl-a-(e)	'he sees / will see'
iñ teheñ noa khEt-(iñ) si- ked-a, gapa onaTak'-(iñ)si-a	'today I ploughed this rice-field, tomorrow I will plough that one'
an-(em) calak'-a	'thou will go'
unkin parkOm-(kin) agu-akad-a	'they two have brought a cot'
rOhOyic' khEtkhOn-(e) rakap 'hEc' - akan-a	'the sower has appeared from the rice-field'

II. **Accusative :** (ϕ) Like nominative, it is also marked in the verb in the shortened form of the pronouns. Only the animate noun and pronouns are marked. Unlike the subject, it comes between the verb root or the tense/aspect marker and the finite /a/. When the animate noun is in the accusative case it is shown in the verb in the shortened forms of the third personal pronoun, singular or non-singular. When the animate pronoun is in the accusative it is shown in the verb by its shortened form. Only in the present indefinite future of the benefactive stem the inanimate noun or pronoun in the accusative is marked by /-k'/ which is tagged on tó the stem. When the verbroots take two objects the direct object is in the accusative and the indirect in the dative. And in that case the dative is always marked in the verb instead of the accusative. While the accusative may be animate or inanimate noun or pronoun the dative is always animate. Example—

iñ uni-ñ ñEl-ked-(e)-a	'I saw him'
uni iñ-e kuli-ked-iñ-a	'he asked me'
iñ am-iñ ñEl-(me)-a	'I will see you'

III. **Instrumental :** The suffix used to mark the instrumental case is /-tE/. used after both animate and inanimate nouns and pronouns, primary and secondary. Example —

Dañ-(tE) tiyok'-mE	'pull down by the stick'
iñ-(tE)-ñ mak'-akan-a	'(it) is cut by me'
uni ona-(tE)-a beret-ked-e-a	'he raised him/her by that (thing)'
uni TuTi-(tE) eẼRẼ TuTi-led-e-a-e	'he pierced the bird with the arrows'
uni sat take- (tE) danra hatao-akad-e-a-e	'he has brought the bullock by seven rupees'
tinak' gOnOñ-(tE)-m hatao-a	'At what price would you take (it)'
TEñgOc 'hOpOm-(tE)-ñ mak' - len-a	'I had cut myself by a small axe'
noa hOR dO ranakap'-(tE) pErEc'-ge-a	'this road is full with ups'

IV. **Dative :** The dative case morpheme /a-/, a prefix, is attached to only animate nouns and pronouns. It is marked in the verb in the form of a prefix being added to the shortened forms of the personal pronouns. Like the object in the accusative case the dative forms of the pronoun come between the root and the finite /a / when the tense marker is zero (ϕ). When the tense/aspect markers occur the case morpheme /a-/ is fused with the tense/aspect markers. The dative forms of the personal pronouns are as follows —

Person		Singular	Dual	Plural
1st	Inclusive	añ	alaṅ	abo
	Exclusive		aliñ	alE
2nd		am	aben/abin	apE
3rd		ae	akin	ako

When the dative is an animate noun it is represented in the verb by /a/ plus the short forms of the third personal pronoun, singular or non-singular. When it is a personal pronoun it is represented by its dative form.

gORO - (añ)-mE 'help me'

iñ ul-iñ Em-(am)-a 'I will give you a mango'

uni lǝi-(ako)-a-e 'he tells/will tell them'

birsǝ uduk'-(ae)-mE 'show Birsa'?

When the dative case morpheme is fused with the tense/aspect markers the infixed forms of the personal pronouns come after the tense/aspect morkers. Thus —

uni lǝi-a-d-iñ-a-e(ad + a + ked) 'he told me'

alaṅ hOR-laṅ ǝgu-a-d- e-a' 'we (incl) brought the man something'

uni alE sim-e-kol-akaw-a-t' iE-a 'he has sent us a cock'

siok'-ko daka-e idi-at'-ko-a 'she took food out to the plough-men'

V. **Ablative :** The ablative case morpheme is /-khOc'/ in the northern dialect and /khOn/ in the southern. /khOn/ is also used sporadically in the northern dialect. /khOn/ with the impersonal suffixes /-ak'/ and /-aṅ/ are also very common in the southern dialect. It is used after both animate and inanimate nouns and pronouns. Thus —

Southern dialect :

dare-(khOnak')-e rakap 'hijuk'-kan-a' 'he is coming up from the water'

raja oRak'-(khOnak')-e dəR-ked-a	'the king fled away from the house'
uni dare-(khOnak') jO-e uyuk 'et' -tahẼc'	'he is plucking fruit down from the tree'
noa jinis-ko-(khOnak') hatao-mE	'take from these things'
am dOsTi-(khOnak') barea-m hatao-a	'you take/will take two from these ten'
dare-(khOn)ãRgon-mE	'come down from the tree'
nəi-(khOn) dak'-iñ əgui-a	'I shall bring/bring water from the river'
səRim-(khOn) ñEl-ok'-kan-a	'it is being seen from the roof'
abo-(khOn) mit' hOR	'one man from us'
OkOe-(khOn) sOpOhOt'-iñ ñam-a	'from whom I shall get help'
phulmoni-(khOn) lokkhi do-e marañ-ge-a	'Lakshmi is older than Phulmani'

Northern dialect :

sikhər-(khOc') tunDi-tE-lE hEc' -en-a	'we came from Sikhar to Tundi'
pukhri-(khOc') rakap 'hijuk'-mE'	'come up from the pond'

VI. **Genetive :** Different methods are employed to form the genitive case in Santali. The uses of suffixes are very common. Sometimes, a zero suffix occurs. Sometimes, the suffixed genitive is dispensed with in favour of a genitive form of the personal pronoun which is incorporated within the verb when the genitive reflects a possessor-possessed relationship. Normally, the kinship terms are used with the short forms of the personal pronouns to make the genitive.

(i) Suffixed Genitive :

a. There are separate suffixes for the genitive depending on whether or not the governed noun is animate or inanimate. In the Southern dialect when the governed noun is animate singular the suffix is /-ic'/. When the governed noun is animate and in the non- singular number the suffix is /-rEn/. There is no such singular-non-singular dichotamy in the Northern dialect where the common suffix is /-rEn/ provided the governed noun is animate. Example—

Southern dialect :

Singular :	*iOkhOn-(ic') gidrə*	'Lakhan's son'
	iñ-(ic') gOc'hOR	'my dead one'
	iñ-(ic') uric'	'my bullock'
	iñ-(ic') gatE	'my friend'
	uni-(ic') oRak'gomke	'his wife'
	nui hOR-(ic') kaDa	'this person's buffalo'
	ac'-(ic') kuRi gidrə	'his daughter'
	apE-(ic') ayo	'your mother'
	unku-(ic') ayo	'their mother'
	iñ-(ic') Dañri	'my cow'
	uni-(ic') bəhu	'his wife'
Plural :	*lOkhOn-(rEn) hOpOn*	'Lakhan's sons'
	iñ-(rEn) gatE	'my friends'

Northern dialect :

am-(rEn) mErOm	'thy goat'
mañjhi-(rEn) hOpOnko	'the headman's sons'
iñ-(rEn) gatE	'my friend'
hola-(rEn) ipil	'yesterday's star/stars'

b. There are various suffixes when the governed noun is inanimate ; they are /-ak' /-aṅ/, /-rEak'/ /-rEaṅ/, /-rEnak'/, /-rEnaṅ/, /-aṅ/, /- rEaṅ/, /-rEnak'/ and /-rEnaṅ/ are exclusively used in the southern dialect while /-ak'/ and /-rEak'/ in the Northern, although the scattered use of /-ak'/ in the southern is not unfound.

/-ak'/ and /-aṅ/ are used with the animate noun or pronoun when the genitive denotes the possessor - possessed relationship. Example—

Northern dialect	Southern dialect	
iñ- (ak') oRak'	*iñ-(aṅ) oRak'*	'my house'
am-(ak') katha	*am-(aṅ katha*	'my word'
hapRamko-(ak') katha	*hapRamko-(aṅ) katha*	'the story of the ancestors'
lOkhOn-(ak')ORak'	*lOkhOn (an) oRak'*	'Lakhan's house'
	iñ-(ak')~(aṅ)katha	'my word'
	uni-(ak') akkriti	'his figure'
	ac'- (aṅ) alo	'his light'
	uni-(ak') jinis	'his thing'

/-rEak'/, /rEaṅ/, /-rEnak'/ and /-rEnaṅ/ are used with the inanimate nouns when the governed noun is also inanimate. The formation of /-rEak'/ and /-rEaṅ/ is made by adding the genitive suffix /-ak'/ or /-aṅ/ for the inanimate to the locative suffix of rest, i.e. /- rE/ Lionel Burrows is quite justified in calling this type of genitive as locative-genitive, as this type of genitive denotes, the belongingness of something to a place. /-rEnak'/ and /-rEnaṅ/ are formed by adding the suffix /-ak'/ or /-aṅ/ to the genitive suffix for the animate i.e. /-rEn/. /-rEak'/ is predominant in the northern dialect while /-rEaṅ/, /-rEnak'/ and /-rEnaṅ/ are used in the southern dialect. Example —

Southern dialect

dare-(rEnak') jo OR *dare-(rEnaṅ) jO*	'fruit of the tree'
bir-(rEnak') dare	'tree of the forest'
Ere katha - (rEnak') mucǝt'	'the end of lie'
oRak' - (rEnaṅ) duǝr	'the opening (for ingress and engress) of the house'
dare-(rEak') Dǝr	'the branch of the tree'
noa-(rEak') dam	'the value of this'

mẼrhẼt (rEnak') - (rEnaṅ) hətiər	'arms of iron'
Northern dialect	
bir-(rEak') dare	'a tree of the forest'
nahEl-(rEak') pal	'the share of a plough'
noa katha-(rEak') buTə	'the beginning of this matter'

(ii) Unmarked gentive or zero genitive : This type of formation is found to express possessor-possessed and kinship relationship. Example—

iñ ayo	'my mother'
ako oRak'	'their house'
alE oRak'	'our house'
lOkhOn hOpOn	'Lekhan's son'

(iii) Genitive incorporated in the verb :

hOpOn-e hEc'-en-(tiñ)-a	'my son came'
nahEl idi- (tiñ)mE	'take away my plough'

The use of this type of genitive is decreasing in favour of the suffixed genitive.

(iv) Genitive expressed by adding the bound forms of the personal pronouns : This is restricted to the kinship terms only. Example —

bOkO- (ñ)	'my younger brother'
misEra-(ñ)	'my younger sister'
Era-(ñ)	'my wife'
eṅga- (t)	'his / someone's mother'
bOkO-(t)	'his / someone's younger brother'

VII. **Locative** : Two suffixes are used to form the locative in Santali, /-rE/ denoting locative of rest and /-tE/ for locative of motion. These are used after the inanimate nouns and pronouns, as the animate nouns and pronouns don't have locative case. Example—

Locative of Rest :

kharaṅ-(rE) 'in the ditch'

rumə - (rE) 'in the handkerchief'

siṅgəR OktO - (rE) 'at night fall'

ato-(rE) 'in the village'

jaṅ-(rE) 'in the bone'

ərsi-(rE) 'in the mirror'

jaṅ-ko-(rE) 'in the bones'

Tukuc'-(rE) 'in the small pot'

dare- (rE) 'on the tree'

cupi- (rE) 'in the tail'

setak'- (rE) 'in the morning

oka-(rE) 'at which place, i.e. where'

topon somOy-(rE) 'at bath time'

cãdo- (rE) 'in the month'

disOm-(rE) 'in the country'

dak'-(rE) 'into the water'

oRak'-(rE) 'in the house'

bin-(rE) 'in the forest'

chatcetan-(rE) 'on the roof'

setoṅ-(rE) 'in the sun'

tala-(rE) 'in the middle'

butə- (rE) 'in the beginning'

jãhã-(rE) 'in any place'

gharOnj-(rE) 'in the household'

nutət'-(rE) 'in the dark'

samaṅ-(rE) 'in front'

gOnOṅ-(rE) 'in the value'

ti- (rE) 'on hand, at hand'

bhitri-(rE) 'inside'

jaṅga- (rE) 'on feet'

ñində-(rE) 'at night'

khEt'-(rE) 'in the field'

bhagolpur-(rE) 'at Bhagalpur'

mOne-(rE) 'in mind'

noa-(rE) 'in this'

ona-(rE) 'in that'

hana-(rE) 'in that yonder'

Locative of Motion :

haT-(rE) 'to the market'

uni bhor-(tE) tiyok'-led-a-e 'he arrived at dawn'

oka-(tE)-m calak'kan-a 'where are you going'

noa kapaT–(tE) calak'-mE 'go through this door'

noa duər-(tE) calak'-mE 'go through this opening'

iskul-(tE) calak'-mE 'go to the school'

nəi-(tE)-ñ calak'-a 'I go/shall go to the river'

tin somOy-(tE)-m calak'a 'at what time you will go'

dare-(tE) dejok'-mE 'climb the tree'

uni raybaric' do oRak'-(tE) - kin əgu-e-a 'they two will bring the Raybaric (negotiator) to the house'

VIII. **Sociative** : The sociative case is formed by adding various postpositions like /tuluc'/, /são/, /sOṅgE/, /saṅ/, /salak'/, /sathe/ and /sElEt'/. Some of the postpositions like /sOṅge/, /são/, and /saṅ/ are also used in combination with the suffix /-tE/ to indicate the same. Example—

uni-iñ-(tulic')-e hEc'-akan-a 'he has come with me'

uni-(tuluc') tahEn-mE 'stay with him'

unku- (tuluc') sEn-Ok'-mE 'go with them'

apat-(sElEt')-ko hEc'-en-a 'they have come with their father'

hOpOn-sElEt' bana eṅga hõ gOc'-led-e-a 'he killed a she-bear along with her cub'

uni-(saõtE) mit'Taṅ alo mEnak'-a 'there is a lamp with him'

uni-hOR- (saõtE) hEc'-len-a 'he came along with a man'

hOpOn-(saõtE) bana eṅga hõ-e gOc'-led-e-a 'he killed a she-bear along with her cub'

alE-(são)hijuk'me 'come with us'

unku ac' baba-(sãotE)-ko hec'-len-a 'they came with their father'

in yu-(são)bajor-iñ calak'-kan-a 'I am going to the market with my mother'

baklak'-(salak') dO alo-pE əgui-a 'do not bring the timber with the bark on'

sagaR-(sElEt')-e calao-en-a 'he went taking a cart along'

pOtOb-(são) seleT hõ ∂gui- mE 'bring a slate along with books'

nui hOR-(salak') tahEn-mE 'stay with this man'

uni-saṅ dejok'-mE 'climb with him'

EtOhOp'-(saṅtE) sereñ hoyuk' - a 'there will be music at the beginning'

phaD-(sOṅgE) 'with the crowd'

sadOm-(sOngEtE) hijuk'-mE 'come along with the pony'

POSTPOSITION :

It is a known fact that the Munda languages are very rich in postpositions and different syntanctic relations are expressed by these. Santali being a Munda language is not an exception. Some of the case-relations are expressed by using different postpositions. Besides case-relations there may be other syntactic relations which are also expressed with the aid of postpositions.

Santali postpositions can be divided into two groups — one denoting syntatic relations including case relations, and the other being used for morphological constructions. A particular postposition may have different grammatical functions, i.e. it may be used to denote either syntactic relation or to form some morphological constructions.

There are certain postpositions which are always bound i.e. their occurrence always depends on free morphemes. There are also certain postpositions which are actually free words but sometimes occur as postpositions as well, i.e. occuring after nominals they express certain syntactic relations. They are made of nouns and verbs with or without a suffix. There is, again, a number of postpositions which are also used as verbs. A good number of postpositions like /sOṅgE/, /sathe/, /sudh∂/, /dhare/ are borrowed from the neighbouring IA. languages like Bengali and Hindi. Dialectal peculiarities in the use of the postpositions are also found. They are to be discussed in the analysis of the respective postpositions.

The postpositions are added either to the nouns and pronouns with or without the number suffixes or to the enclitic definitives added to these. Some of them are also added to the infinitives. Some are also used after the genitive. A few postpositions are also used after a complete phrase and even after a sentence. The postpositions which are discussed elsewhere, while discussing the case or the degree of adjectives, are not touched upon here unless they express some other functions and meanings.

The postpositions are discussed below—

(i) /ThEn/ThEc'/ : It conveys the sense 'nearby, beside (something or somebody or place)' /ThEn/ is common in the Southern dialect while /ThEc'/ is in the Northern. Example—

iñ-(ThEn)menak'-a 'It is with me'

ona alo-(ThEn)-e seTer-enkhan-ge uni biñ dO hətiar-tE-e gOc'-en-a 'having been reached near the light that snake was killed by the weapon'

uni-ak' bOhOk'-(ThEn) tahẼkan-a mit'Tan rupəkəThi ar sona kət-hi 'there was a silver stick and a golden stick near his head'

uni budhi-(ThEn) colo -bon 'go before that old lady'

mãjhi-(ThEn)-e calak's 'he will go to the village headman'

əliñ-(ThEn) 'with us'

OkOe- (ThEn) noa-ñ ñam-a 'with whom shall I get it'

iñ am-(ThEn) noa katha ləi- ləgit'-iñ hEc'len-a 'I came to tell you this'

uni ato mãjhi-(ThEn) sOpOhOt'-e ñam- a 'he will get help with the village headman'

uni ac'baba-(ThEn)-a tahEn-a 'he stays with his father'

uni-(ThEnrE)mena-e-a 'he is with him'

N.S. noa-dO OkOe-(ThEn) manak's 'this is with whom'

(ii) /sEn/sEc'/ a postposition denoting direction./sEn/ and /sEc'/ are used indiscriminately, no dialectal feature can be had from the distribution of these. Example—

gOra-(sEc')-gecdhar henak'-a 'there is sharpness in all directions'

nəidak'-(sEc') 'towards the river water'

bir-(sEc') 'towards the forest'

oka-(sEc') 'to which direction'

bir-(sEn) 'towards the forest'

buru-(sEn) 'towards the mountain'

ato-(sEn) 'towards the village'

(iii) /lǝgit'/lagat'/ : The postpositions are used to express purposes and intention after all nouns, pronouns and infinitives. They are also sometimes used in combination with the suffix /- tE/, hence /lǝgit'tE/, /lagat'tE/ with the same meaning. /lǝgit'/ with /lǝgit'tE/ is predominant in the Northern dialect while both /lǝgit'/ with /lǝgit'tE/ and /lagat'/ with /lagat'tE/ are prevalent in the Southern, the use of the one or the other being dependent on the individual choice. Example—

uni rajhOpOn- (lǝgit') do bislǝou ǝgu-ad-e-a-e 'he brought poisonous sweet for the prince'

iñ am noa katha meta-m-(lǝgit' tE)- ñ hEc' -len-a 'I came for telling you this word'

nEs dO uni ac' -(lǝgit')-e ǝgu-akawn-a 'this year he has brought for himself'

Take-(lǝgit')-iñ hEc' - akan-a 'I have come for money'

am-(lǝgit')-iñ hEc' -akan-a 'I have come for you'

Taka-ñam-(lǝgit')-iñ hec' - akan-a 'I have come to have money'

iñ nui-(lǝgit' tE) toa-ñ hatao-ed-a 'I am taking milk for drinking'

ǝkhriñ-(lǝgit') 'for selling'

uduk' -(lǝgit') 'for showing'

kǝuDi-(lǝgit')-iñ hEc' - akan- a 'I have come for money'

cet' - (lǝgit') 'for what purpose'

topo-(lǝgit') 'for the purpose of bathing'

payrak' -(lǝgit') 'for the purpose of swimming'

benao-(lǝgit') 'for making'

gidra-(lǝgit') 'for the hot'

sap' -(lǝgit') 'for catching'

alE-(lǝgit') 'for us'

Southern dialect :

uni ac'- (lagat' tE)ñEl-en-a-e 'he say for himself'

am-(lagat')-iñ hEc'-akan-a 'I have come for you'

(iv) /modre/ (var./mudre/) : 'among', locative of *mod* 'middle'. The borrowed postposition from Bengali /moddhe/ with /-rE/, hence /moddherE/ is also used in the same sense. Example—

apE-(moddherE) jāhāe-ge lOgOn hijuk'-pE 'any one of you come quickly'

noako-(modre) kombRo mena-e-a 'there is thief among these persons'

apE-(moddherE) jāhāe-ge lOgOn hijuk'- pE 'any one of you come quickly'

noako-(modre) hatao-joṅ-me 'take from among these things'

noko-(modre) kombRo mena-e-a 'there is thief among these persons'

apE-(moddherE) jāhāe-ge lOgOn hijuk -pE 'any one of you come quickly'

alE-(moddhe) jāhāe mit' hoR 'any one of us'

(v) /dharerE/ : locative suffix /-rE/being added to /dhare/ 'side', hence by the side' (cp. Bengali *dhare* 'by the side'). *bir-(dharerE)* 'by the side of the forest'.

(vi) /dhərbic' dhəRic'/ : Convey the sense 'till, until, upto' etc. denoting both time as well as space dimension. The variant forms of these postpositions are /həbic'/ and /həRic'/. They are used after nouns of place, after inanimate indefinite interrogative and inanimate indefinite pronouns and in these cases the space dimension is indicated by the postposition. After infinitives the time dimension is specified. The same time dimension is specified when it is used after interrogative adjectives. Example—

curə-(dhəRic') 'upto the top (of the mountain)'

buru-(dhəbic') 'upto the mountain'

bir-(həbic') 'upto the forest'

nəi-(həRic') 'upto the river'

uni əuRi hijuk'-(dhəbic') okatE- hõ alom calak'a 'do not go to anywhere until he comes'

gujuk'-(dhəbic') 'until death'

jiwet'-iñ tahEn-(dhəbic') 'till I live'

oka-(həbic') 'upto which'

jãhã-(dhəbic') 'upto any (place)'

tin-(həbic') 'until what time'

(vii) /*bhitər-bhitri* / : 'inside', with locative suffix of rest, /-rE/, /bhitərrE/, /bhitrirE/, hence 'inside, within, among'. Example—

oRak'-(bhitrirE) men-e-a 'he is there in the house'

satdin-(bhitrirE) 'within seven days'

alE-(bhitrirE)mit' hOR 'one man among us'

dak'-(bhitrirE) ona dO cet' laRak'kana 'what is moving in the water'

With the suffix for locative of motion /-tE/, hence /bhitərtE/ /bhitritE/ they express 'to the inside'.

uni oRak'-(bhitərtE) seTerok'-a-e OR uni oRak'- (bhitritE) seTerok'-a-e 'he will enter into the inside of the house'

(viii) /tala-rE/ : locative of /tala/ 'middle, centre', hence in the middle'. Example—

oRak'-(talarE) duRup'-akan-a-e 'he is sitting in the middle of the house'

(ix) /latar-rE/ : locative of /latar/ 'below' and conveys the locative sense used only with the noun. Example—

dhiri-(latarrE) 'under a stone'

Ot-(latarrE) 'under the earth'

dare-(latarrE) 'under the tree'

jaṅga-(latarrE) 'under the feet'

(x) /cetan-rE/ : locative of /cetan/ 'above, top', used only with noun to indicate a locative sense. Example—

oRak'-(cetanrE) 'on the house'

dare-(cetanrE) 'on the tree'

duṅri-(cetenrE) 'on the hill'

(xi) /cOT/ : 'top', always used with the locative suffixes, /-tE/ when movement is marked and /-rE/ when rest, to carry a locative sense, hence /coTtE/, /cOTrE/. It is used with nouns only. Example—

buru- (cOTtE)lE sEn-akan-a 'we have gone to the top of the mountain'

dare-(cOTrE) menak'-a 'it is on the top of the tree'

(xii) /leka/ : adjectival and adverbial postposition meaning 'like'. It is added to all kinds of nouns and pronouns and even to adverbs. With the suffix /-tE/ the way of action is specified. Example—

tərup'- (leka) 'like a leopard'

onka-(leka) 'like thus'

cet'-(leka) 'like what'

nui-(leka) hOR kana-e 'he is a man like this person'

OkOe-(leka) mena-e-a 'what is he like'

noṅka-(leka) alo-m ləi-a 'do not say like this'

oka-(lekatE) hõ noa dO alom EmOk'-a 'you would not give it by any means'

noa-(lekatE) onko dO hORo-ko rOhOy-ed-a 'they are sowing paddy in this way'

(xiii) /atE/ : 'taking along with'.

uni ləThi- (atE) taRam-ed-a-e 'he is walking taking a stick along'

uni ac'rEn gidrə-(atE) dəR-akad-a-e 'he has run away taking his children along'

(xiv) /sOmmonddhe/ sOmpOrkOtE/ : 'about', borrowed from Bengali, used with the genitive or the root itself. Example—

uni amak'- (sOmmondhe) cet' hõ bako lði- a-e 'he will not tell anything about you'

ato-(sOmpOrkOtE) 'about the village'

(xv) /pOre/ : 'after', (cp. Bengali *pOre* 'after')

ona-(pOre) 'after that'

(xvi) /hOtEc'tE/ (var. hOtEtE) : 'for, by, due', indicating instrumentality.

dak' bOdE-(hOtEc'tE) bañ topo-len-a 'I did not bathe due to dirty water'

uni ruðk'-(hotEc'tE) ba-e hEc'-akan-a 'he has not come due to having fever'

uni-(hOtEc'tE) calao bañ ganok'-a 'going will not be done by him'

ona- (hOtEc'tE) bðñ calak'-a 'I shall not go for that'

mit'ghðRic'-(hOtEc'tE) ñuruk' ñuruk'-tE bancao-en-a-e 'he was saved from falling for one minute'

ruðk'kan-(hOtEc'tE) 'due to having fever'

Taka ñamok'-(hOtEc'tE) 'for having money'

(xvii) /tuluc'/ : denotes being with, association with, meeting with, from the most casual to the most intimate :

sEnOk'-(tuluc')-e jðpit' idi-ed-a 'he sleeps as he walks'

uni calak'-(tuluc')-e mEn-led-a 'he said as he walked'

(xviii) /katE/ : Purely a gerundial postposition, meaning 'having done' but is also used after simple demonstrative interrogative and inanimate indefinite demonstrative pronouns, nouns and adjectives with an adverbial force. Example —

ruðR hEc'-(katE) 'having returned'

hEc'-(katE) 'having come'

lði-(katE) 'having told'

rakap'-(katE) 'having risen'

dOhO-(katE) 'having kept'

ãjom-(katE) 'having heard'

Ol-(katE) 'having written'

phasiara(katE) hatao-ked-a-e 'he got possession of it deceitfully'

mit'Taka-(katE) Em-ako-m 'give them one rupee each'

babar-(katE) kol-ket-ko-a-e 'he sent them out in couples'

ona-(katE) 'in that way'

In continuing a narrative it indicates 'then, 'after this'.

inə-(katE)-ko ãRgon-a 'after that they harrow it'

(xix) /mEntE/ : *mEn'* 'say' + /tE? (lit. 'by saying') 'for the purpose of'.

dhup-(mEntE) saDe-kan-a 'making a thud sound'

ghir-mEntE hijuk'-mE 'come slowly'

cet'-(mEntE) calao-en-a-e 'for what purpose did he go?'

Thenga-(mEntE) mak' əgu-akat'-a-e 'he cut and brought it in order to make a stick'

(xx) /iətE/ : 'on account; owing to, due to', used after nouns, pronouns and infinitives. Example —

ona-(iətE) 'therefore'

am-(iətE)-ñ hEc -akan-a 'I have come because of you'

ədi hOR-(iətE) ba-e sor-len-a 'she did not come near on account of the multitude of people'

ru-(iətE) ba-e hEc -len-a 'he did not come on account of fever'

(xxi) /tayOm/ : 'behind, back'.

iñ - (tayOm) 'after that'

ENCLITIC DEFINITIVES :

Santali possesses two suffixes — one for the noun and the infinitives and the other for the pronouns, which are used after nouns, infinitives and pronouns other than personal to define the nature of the object referred to. The suffixes when added to nouns and pronouns become a part of them, the number and case affixes and postpositions coming after them. They are called then the definitives as they are used only when the object is specified. Where the object is unspecified the definitive is not used.

Two definitives are /tEt'/ for noun and infinitive and /Tak'/ for pronouns. Example—

hOpOn-(tEt')	'the son'
dər-(tEt')	'the branch'
gEt'-(tEt')	'the cutting'
hOr-(tEt')	'the path'
hErEl-(tEt')	'the husband'
nui-(Tak')	'the one hare' (animate)
noa-(Tak')	'the thing here'
nii-(Tak')	'this very one' (one animate)
hana-(Tak')	'that very one' (inanimate)
oka-(Tak')	'which very one' (do)
jāhā-(Tak')	'any thing' (do)
OkOe-(Tak')	'which one' (animate)
niə-(Tak')	'this thing' (particular)
oka-(Tak')	'which one' (inanimate)
bOkOt-(tEt')-tako	'his brothers'
bəhut'-(tEt')	'his wife'
eṅgat-(tEt')	'his mother'
gəi-(tEt')	'he cow'
hilit-(tEt')	'his sister-in-law'
dadat- (tEt')	'his elder brother'
əjit- (tEt')	'his elder sister'
apat-(tEt')	'his father'
kakat- (tEt')	'his uncle'
apat-(tEt')-tEko	'their fathers'
ac'-(tEt')	'he himself'
jinis- (tEt')	'the thing'
balat-(tEt')	'his co-parent-in-law'

4

CONJUGATIONAL MORPHEMES

The Santali verb is defined by the fact that it takes tense and/or aspect markers with or without the markers for the active and neutral, modal markers, personal terminations, marker for the finiteness of action and gerundial suffix. The words which denote action, event or condition are not the ones treated as verbs but any word is treated as such provided it takes the above markers. The verb with the finite marker is treated as finite[1] and without this and with the gerundial suffix is treated as non- finite.

Santali verb structure may be shown in the following diagram.

Root : The roots from which the verbs are formed can be classified into three groups — transitive, intransitive and transitive- intransitive, according to the markers they take for the active or neutral along with tense/aspect markers and according to their potential capacity of taking object infixes.

Transitive verbroots :

idi '(to) take away' | *sap'* '(to) catch'
isin '(to) cook' | *kiriñ* '(to) buy'
ir '(to) reap' | *əkhriñ* '(to) sell'
ñam '(to) get' | *dOhO* '(to) keep, put down'

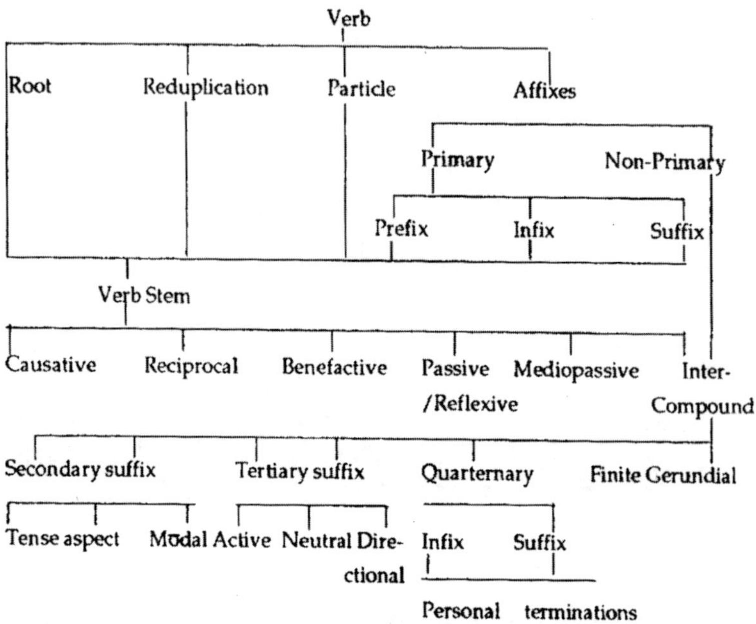

ñEl '(to) see' *hatao* '(to) take'
dal '(to) beat' *jəpit'* '(to) sleep, make sleep'
tOl '(to) bind' *rOhOy* '(to) sow'
cas '(to) cultivate' *rapak'* '(to) burn'
dak' '(to) ruin' *atkir* '(to) steal'
jOm '(to) eat'
tuñ '(to) shoot with bow and arrow *EhOp'* '(to) begin'
rOR '(to) speak'
rak' '(to) cry' *sendra* '(to) hunt, seek'
mak' '(to) cut' *añjOm/ãjOm* '(to) hear'
cak' '(to) learn, teach' *kuli* '(to) ask'
dəR '(to) run' *kami* '(to) work'
gOṅ '(to) give a daughter in marriage, respond' *sap'* (to) catch'
kurumuTu '(to) try'
toa '(to) give milk'
bicər '(to) judge' *gupi* '(to) tend cattle'

dapal '(to) cover'	*Er* '(to) sow'
ñu '(to) drink'	*EgEr* '(to) scold' (used by women)
utu '(to) prepare curry'	
savay '(to) have a full supply of rain'	*rOhEt'* / *ruhEt'* '(to) scold' (by men)
pañja/pãja '(to) trace'	
oar '(to) take, pull out of water'	*uyuk'* '(to) cover with cloth'
sin '(to) shut'	*gidi* '(to) throw away'
thekao '(to) push into fire'	*akao* '(to) draw picture'
deri '(to) delay'	*ataṅ* '(to) spread out to receive'
bilom '(to) delay'	
khema '(to) spend time with joy'	*galmaroa* '(to) converse'
si '(to) plough'	
kurpar '(to) arrange for wrong purpose'	*taṅgi* '(to) wait'
hudis '(to) think'	*ghaet* '(to) bind a knot'
ORhẼ '(to) sing in praise'	*tiyok'* '(to) reach'
ãRgo '(to) be pregnant'	*uyuk* '(to) bring down'
baDa/*baRa* '(to) know'	*həTiṅ* '(to) divide'
laga '(to) chase, drive away'	*la* '(to) dig'
bErhOn '(to) earn'	*cesTa* '(to) try'
sereñ '(to) sing'	*taram* '(to) walk'
tovak' '(to) throw down'	
atin '(to) tend cattle'	*lo* '(to) lift water'
sarEc' '(to) exceed'	
ak' '(to) bow'	*saprao* '(to) edit'
jãvãy '(to) give a daughter in marriage'	*hiriṅ* '(to) forget'
jOrao '(to) link'	*ñum* '(to) name'
Or '(to) draw, pull'	*dis* '(to) remember, be conscious of'
pOtOm '(to) cover with winnow'	
tiə/*tiək'* '(to) bend'	
banam '(to) play fiddle'	*ru* '(to) sound'

gEt' '(to) cut'
tin '(to) stone'
don '(to) jump'
ran '(to) treat medically'
hEi/(hen) '(to) take on the lap'
arjao '(to) earn'
Em '(to) give'
lәi '(to) tell'
uduk' '(to) show'
hOhO '(to) call'
gORO '(to) help'
dul '(to) pour'
әris '(to) bear malice'
bEṅgEt' '(to) watch'
chitkәu '(to) sprinkle'
dEc' '(to) ascend'

OrOṅ '(to) blow flute'
bhEja '(to) send'
tam '(to) beat'
EaEt' '(to) cover with winnow'
rikә '(to) try'
cal '(to) give'
mEn '(to) say'
әgu '(to) bring'
rOR '(to) speak'
kol/kul '(to) send'
bәgi '(to) leave'

jut '(to) make'
Ol '(to) write'
calao '(to) go'
unum '(to) submerge'

Intransitive verbroots:

bEt' '(to) cover the eyes with palm/put on a lid'
sEn '(to) go'
hEc' '(to) come'
um '(to) take bath'
seTer '(to) arrive'
bOlO '(to) enter'
teṅgo/tiṅgu '(to) stand'
hoi '(to) be'
ruә '(to) get fever'
parOm '(to) cross cover'
payra '(to) swim'
Dubuc '(to) pop head under water'
raṅgao '(to) get angry'

tuluc' '(to) be associated with; be along with'
rәskә '(to) rejoice'
laṅgao/laṅga '(to) be tired'
hәsur '(to) set'
phEO '(to) get down'
paRao '(to) fall'
rEar '(to) cool'

at' '(to) lose'
әcur '(to) turn'
saOe '(to) ring'

joRon '(to) be joined'
topo '(to) bathe'

khOc' '(to) seek'

dhurəu '(to) begin, start'

ruəR '(to) return'

onDok '(to) come out'

j r '(to) drop'

ñir '(to) run away'

setOri '(to) come out'

gOc' '(to) die, kill'

OmOn '(to) sprout'

ObOr '(to) lie down (animate)'

caco '(to) walk' (Children)

ãkgo '(to) descend'

konDel '(to) fall'

duRup' '(to) sit/make sit'

uDəu/uRəu '(to) fly, make fly'

Transitive-Intransitive Verb roots:

ap' '(to) alight, make alight'

rakap' '(to) rise, ascend, pull somebody/thing up'

paRhao '(to) read, teach'

pErEc' '(to) be full, fill'

caba '(to) end, finish (temporarily)'

rəput' '(to) break, be broken'

beret' '(to) get up, lift'

oDok'/oDon/onDok' '(to) come out, expel'

gitic' '(to) lie down, lay down'

bancao '(to) be saved, save'

busək' '(to) be born, give birth' (of dog)

ñur/ñuru/ñurhə '(to) fall, fell'

burum '(to) lie down, make lied down (of animal)'

bapla '(to) marry, give to marriage'

bhindər/bhĩdər '(to) fall down, fell down'

STEM FORMATION

Causative/Permissive stem : The morphological processes employed to form causative/permissive stems is prefixation and suffixation. Of these, suffixation is employed for all types of roots — transitive, intransitive and transitive-intransitive, and reciprocal stems but prefixation is restricted to two transitive roots only. These two roots can be used in combination with suffix but never in combination with both the processes.

The difference between the causative and the permissive lies in the case status of the person acted upon, though they are formed with the same formatives. In the causative, the person caused, i.e. acted upon, is in the accusative while in the permissive the person acted upon is in the dative.

The suffix for the causative/permissive varies in phonological shape in the two dialects. In the northern, the formative is /- oco/ (also /aco/) and in the southern it is /-hOcO/, while the prefix is uniformly /a-/ in both.

By prefixing /a-/ : This is restricted to the two transitive roots *jOm* 'eat and *ñu* 'drink'. They are also used in combination with the suffix /-oco/- /-hOcO/.

Prefixation

Northern	Southern	
jOm 'eat' *aj* 'feed'	*jOmoco*	*jOmhOcO* id.
ñu 'drink' *añu* 'make drink'	*ñuoco*	*ñuhOcO* id.

By suffixing /-oco/ - /hOcO/ :

(i) To transitive roots :

Northern		Southern	
dal 'beat'	*daloco*	*dalhOcO*	'cause to beat, allow to beat'
mEn 'say'	*mEnoco*	*mEnhOcO*	'cause to say, allow to say'
ñEl 'see'	*ñEloco*	*nElhOcO*	'cause to see, allow to see'
tiə 'pick up from tree'	*tiəoco*	*tiəhOcO*	'cause to pick up, allowed to pick up'
uyuk' 'bring down'	*uyuk' oco*	*uyuk' hOcO*	'cause to bring down, allow to bring down'
ran 'treat medically'	*ranoco*	*ranhOcO*	'cause to treat medically, allow to treat medically'
bicər 'judge'	*bicəroco*	*bicərhOcO*	'cause, allow to judge'

(ii) To intransitive roots :

Northern		Southern
sEn 'go'	*sEnoco*	*sEnhOcO* 'cause, allow to go'

calao 'go'	*calaooco*	*calaohOcO*	'cause, allow to go'
hEc' 'come'	*hEc* 'oco'	*hEc'hOcO*	'cause, allow to come'

(iii) To the transitive-intransitive roots :

gitic' 'lie, lay'	*gitic'oco*	*gitic'hOcO*	'cause to allow to lie, lay'
duRup' 'sit, make sit'	*durup'hco*	*duRup' hOcO*	'cause to allow to sit, make sit'
pErEc' 'be full, fill'	*pErEc'oco*	*pErEc'hOcO*	'cause to/ allow to be full, to fill'
gOc' 'die/kill'	*gOc'oco*	*gOc'hOcO*	'cause to/ allow to die, kill'

(iv) To reciprocal stems :

ñEpEl 'see each other, meet'	*ñEpEloco*	*ñEpElhOcO*	'cause to/allow to see each other, meet'
ñapam 'get together, meet'	*ñapamoco*	*ñapamhOcO*	'cause to/ allow to mee

BENEFACTIVE STEM

The benefactive stem is formed by suffixing /-ka/ to the transitive and transitive-intransitive roots. When added to the transitive-intransitive roots the transitive meaning is prominent. The stem indicates an action done for somebody else.

tOl 'bind'	*tOlka* 'bind (for somebody)'
gitic' 'lay'	*gitic'ka* 'lay (for somebody)'
depal 'cover'	*depalka* 'cover (for somebody)'
dOhO 'keep'	*dOhOka* 'keep (for somebody)'
duRup' 'make sit'	*duRup'ka* 'make sit (for somebody)'
rOhOy 'sow'	*rOhOyka* 'sow (for somebody)'
kəmi 'work'	*kəmika* 'work (for somebody)'

dal 'thrash (paddy)'	*dalka* 'thrash (for somebody)'
pOtOm 'cover'	*pOtOmka* 'cover (for somebody)'

The benefactive stem suffix, in the southern Santali is /-kak'/ when there is no animate object or no object at all. In case the animate object is infixed the final /k'/ is replaced by the pronominal infixes otherwise bare /-kak'/ is used. In the northern dialect, it is invariably /-ka/. The conjugation of the benefactive in the Northern and Southern dialects go thus :

Northern	Southern
Dañra tOlka-e-mE	*gidrə dOhOka-E-mE*
bullock-bind(ben.)-3po-you	child - keep (ben.)
'bind the bullock'	'keep the child'
dapalka - m	*kəmikak' - mE*
cover (ben.) - you	work (ben.) - you 'work'
	bin gOc'ka -e - mE
	snake-kill (ben.) -3rd p r. obj-you 'kill the snake'
hoRo dalka-m	*silpiñ sinkak' - mE*
paddy-thrash(ben.)-you 'thrash paddy'	door - close (ben.) - you 'close the door'

RECIPROCAL STEM

The morphological processes employed to form the reciprocal stem is infixation and suffixation. Both the processes are restricted to the transitive and transitive-intransitive roots, though in the latter case the transitive meaning is prominent.

a. *Infixation* : The infix /-pV^r-/ is inserted after the first vowel of the root, the vowel of the infix being the same root vowel after which the insertion takes place, hence, the vowel of the infix is represented as V^r

dal 'beat'	*dapal* 'beat each other'
Em 'give'	*EpEm* 'give each other'
ləi 'tell'	*ləpəi* 'tell each other'
Or 'draw, pull'	*OpOr* 'draw each other'
gEr 'bite'	*gEpEr* 'bite each other'

ñEl 'see'	*ñEpEl* 'see each other, meet'
tuñ 'pierce (with arrow)'	*tupuñ* 'pierce each other (with arrow)'
rOR 'speak'	*rOpOR* 'speak to each other, gossip, quarrel'
mak' 'cut'	*mapak'* 'cut each other'
rOk' 'pierce through'	*rOpOk'* 'pierce each other through'
Ol 'write'	*OpOl* 'write to each other'
tOl 'bind'	*tOpOl* 'bind each other'
tul 'draw water'	*tupul* 'draw water for each other'
cal 'give'	*capal* 'give each other'
EgEr 'scold, abuse'	*EpEgEr* 'scold each other, quarrel'
hOhO 'call'	*hOpOhO* 'call each other'
taṅgi 'wait'	*tapaṅgi* 'wait for each other'
kuli 'ask'	*kupuli* 'ask each other'
galmarao 'chat'	*gapalamarao* 'gossip'
landa 'laugh'	*lapanda* 'laugh together'
uduk' 'show'	*upuduk'* 'show each other'

b. *Suffixation* :

(i) By suffixing /-ok'/ to the transitive and the transitive-intransitive roots :

gEr 'bite'	*gErOk'* 'bite each other'
EgEr 'scold, abuse'	*EgErOk* 'scold, abuse each other'
dal 'beat'	*dalok'* 'beat each other'
taṅgi 'wait'	*taṅgik'* 'wait for each other'
hOhO 'call'	*hOhOk'* 'call each other'

(ii) Sometimes the reciprocal stem is also formed by adding /- jOṅ/ to a restricted number of transitive roots, like,

ləi 'tell'	*ləijoṅ* 'tell each other'
hOhO 'call'	*hOhOjOṅ* 'call each other'
Em 'give'	*EmjOṅ* 'give each other'

The infixation is the only process of forming the reciprocal stem in the Southern dialect while in the Northern dialect there is an optional variation between this process of infixation and the process of suffixation. And this suffix-type of reciprocal formation is particularly used by the male teenagers while the grown up men and the women particularly cling to the first process.

The suffixed reciprocal stems, unlike infixed ones, are congugated only in simple present/future, present and past progressive and in the imperative mood. In other tenses and moods, the simple roots are congugated, while the context shows whether it is reciprocal or not.

Iterative/intensive Stem

This is formed by reduplicating the initial consonants along with the accompanying vowels or the initial vowels, if the roots begin with a consonant or a vowel respectively, as the case may be. This is restricted to the transitive roots and to two intransitive roots only. Both the iterative and the intensive functions are performed by the same stem, the context determining whether the iterative or intensive meaning is hinted upon.

(i) With the Transitive roots:

gEt' 'cut'	*gEgEt'*
ñEl 'see'	*ñEñEl*
mak' 'cut'	*mamak'*
dal 'beat'	*dadal*
rOR 'speak'	*rOrOR*
tOl 'bind'	*tOtOl*
dəR 'run'	*dOdOR*
jək' 'sweep'	*jOjOk'*
rək' 'pierce'	*rərək'*
dak' 'rain'	*dadak'*
rak' 'cry'	*rarak'*
cas 'cultivate'	*cacas*
ñu 'drink'	*ñu*
tuñ 'pierce'	*tutuñ*
gəc' 'kill'	*gəgəc'*
tot' 'pack'	*totot'*
ñam 'get'	*ñañam*
səṅ 'measure'	*səsəṅ*
gEr 'bite'	*gEgEr*
Or 'pull/draw'	*əər*

ir 'reap'	*iir*
Er 'sow'	*EEr*
jəm 'eat'	*jəjəm*
si 'plough'	*sisi*
Ol 'write'	*ool*
Em 'give'	*EEm*
benao 'make'	*bebenao/bebnao*
banam 'play on violin'	*babanam/babnam*
hatao 'take'	*hahatao*
kuli 'ask'	*kukuli/kukli*
sap' 'catch'	*sasap'*

(ii) Only two intransitive roots are found undergoing reduplication to form an iterative / intensive stem :

sEn 'go' *sEsEn* 'go intensively repeatedly'

ñir 'run' *ñiñir* 'run again and again, run persistently'

The roots with the initial consonants followed by diphthongs reduplicate their initial consonants along with the first components of the diphthongs :

ləi 'tell' *lələi* 'tell over and again, reiterate'

Bodding has mentioned a process of forming the 'performative base', here iterative / intensive, by infixing /-k'/ after the initial vowel of the root,[2] but this type of formation is not returned in my data either from the Northern or from the Southern.

The iterative / intensive stems are conjugated in the simple present future, present and past progressive and cannot take any object infix.

Medio-passive Stem

The morphological process employed to form a medio-passive stem is to suffix /-jOṅ/ to the transitive roots, to a limited number of intransitive and transitive-intransitive roots, the intransitive meaning being prominent in the latter case. The stem thus formed denotes an action meant for the actor doer himself.

(i) With the transitive roots :

dal 'beat, thrash' *daljOṅ* 'beat, thrash for self'

əgu 'bring'	*əgujoṅ* 'bring for self'
kəmi 'work'	*kəmijOṅ* 'work for self'
ñEl 'see'	*ñEljOṅ* 'see for self'
rəskə 'rejoice'	*rəskəjOṅ* 'rejoice for self'
ir 'reap'	*irjOṅ* 'reap for self'
uyuk' 'bring'	*uyuk'jOṅ* 'bring for self'
ru 'play on drum	*rujOṅ* 'to play on drum for self'
OrOṅ 'play on flute'	*OrOṅjOṅ* 'to play on flute for self'
sẼra 'learn'	*sẼrajOṅ* 'learn for self'
gEr 'bite'	*gErjOṅ* 'bite for self'

(ii) With the intransitive roots :

ñir 'run away'	*ñirjOṅ* 'run away to save onself'
calao 'go'	*caleojOṅ* 'go for self'

(iii) With the transitive-intransitive roots:

gitic' 'lie'	*gitic'jOṅ* 'lie for self'
duRup' 'sit'	*durup'jOṅ* 'sit for self'

This suffixed stem is conjugated in the simple present / future, present and past progressive and in the imperative mood: in other tenses and moods the simple root replaces the stem.

Passive/Reflexive Stem

The suffix for the passive and reflexive stems is /-ok'/. It is added to the transitive roots and transitive-intransitive roots in which the transitive meaning is prominent and to the causative stem to make the passive and to the transitive roots to make a reflexive as well. There is no formal difference within the verb between the passive and the reflexive, the context alone determining whether passive or reflexive is involved.

(i) Passive from transitive and transitive-intransitive roots :

ñam 'get'	*ñamok'* 'be got, gotten'
ñEl 'see'	*ñElOk* 'be seen'
Em 'give'	*EmOk'* 'be given'
dal 'beat'	*dalok'* 'be beaten'
EhOp' 'start'	*EhObOk'* 'be started'

isin 'cook'	*isinok'* 'be cooked'
añj m/ãjOm 'hear'	*añjOmok' / ãjOmok'* 'be heard'
rOhOy 'sow'	*rOhOyok'* 'be sown'
gOc' 'kill'	*gujuk' / gojok'* 'be killed'

(ii) Passive from causative stem :

ranocó/hOcO 'cause to medicate'	*ranocok'/ranhOcOk'* 'be caused to medicate'
jOmoco/hOcO 'cause to eat'	*jOmocok'/jOmhOcOk'* 'be caused to eat'

(iii) Reflexive from transitive roots :

Ol 'write'	*OlOk'* 'write oneself'
Em 'give'	*EmOk'* 'give oneself'
ñEl 'see'	*ñElok'* 'see oneself'
Or 'draw, pull'	*OrOk'* 'draw or pull oneself'
mak' 'cut'	*magok'* 'cut oneself'
ir 'reap'	*irok'* 'reap oneself'
dal 'beat'	*dalok'* 'beat oneself'
gEr 'bite'	*gErOk'* 'bite oneself'

Passive/Reflexive stem is conjugated in the simple present/future, present and past progressive and in the imperative mood, in other tenses and moods the simple root is conjugated.

Compound Stem

Juxtaposition of two transitive roots :

sendra 'search'	+ *ñam* 'get, find'	*sendrañam* 'search and get'
kəmi 'work'	+ *dare* 'be able'	*kəmidare* 'able to work'
Em 'give'	+ *dare* 'be able'	*Emdare* 'able to give'
mak' 'cut'	+ *əgu* 'bring'	*mak'əgu* 'cut and bring'
ñEl 'see'	+ *ñam'* 'find'	*ñElñam* 'see and find'

Juxtaposition of two intransitive roots :

rakap' 'ascend'	+ *hEc'* 'come'	*rakap'hEc'* 'ascend and come'
ñRgo 'descend'	+ *hEc'* 'come'	*ãrgohEc'* 'descend and come'
ruəR 'return'	+ *hEc'* 'come'	*ruəRhEc'* 'come back'

Juxtaposition of an intransitive root and a transitive root :

sEn 'go' + *dare* 'be able' *sEndare* 'able to go'

Juxtaposition of a root and an adverbial particle:

ñir 'run away'	+ *bara*	*ñirbara* 'run about'
dəR 'run'	+ *bara*	*dəRbara* 'run about'
dal 'beat'	+ *gOt'*	*dalgOt'* 'beat up'
kəmi 'work'	+ oTo (N.S)[3] ḥot (S.S.)[4]	*kəmioTo* / kamih t
sEn 'go'	+ *bara*	*Enbara* 'go about'

By a reclassification of the above stems, two groups, henceforth called active and neutral, may be set up depending on the formative elements added to the tense/aspect markers and on the potential capacity of taking objects. The first group, henceforth called active stems, consists of the following:

(i) all transitive roots;

(ii) all transitive-intransitive roots when the transitive meaning is prominent;

(iii) causative-permissive stems;

(iv) benefactive stems;

(v) compound stem consisting of two transitive roots;

(vi) compound stems in which the second element is an adverbial particle.

The second group, henceforth called neutral stems, consists of the following :

(i) all intransitive roots;

(ii) all transitive - intransitive roots when the intransitive meaning is prominent;

(iii) reciprocal stems;

(iv) passive / reflexive stems;

(v) medio-passive stems; and

(vi) compound stems consisting of two intransitive roots.

Iterative / intensive stems are not included in any of the above groups as, when they are conjugated in the simple present/future, present and past progressive and in the imperative mood no overt marker for the active or neutral occurs and they do not admit of any object infix. Another point to note is that the causative / permissive stems are always active irrespective of whether they are formed from the transitive or intransitive roots. The formation of the reciprocal and the benefactive is restricted to the transitive roots, but while the former is always neutral the latter is always active. The passive is always neutral whether it is formed from the transitive or transitive-intransitive roots. The compound stems are active or neutral depending on the transitivity or intransitivity of the last element of the compound. The transitive-intransitive roots are included in both depending on which counterpart (transitive or intransitive) of the root is specified.

Morphophonological Changes

Morphophonological changes in the stem suffixes.

(i) The initial vowel of the passive-reflexive-(reciprocal) suffix /ok'/ is elided when it is added to roots and stems ending in a vowel :

hOhO+ /-ok'/= *hOhOk'*

tańgi+ /-ok'/= *tangik'*

(ii) o of /ok'/ becomes /O/ when it is added to roots with E and O :

gEr+ /-ok'/= *gErOk'*

EgEr+ /-ok'/= *EgErOk'*

ñEl+ /-ok'/= *nElOk'*

Ol+ /-ok'/= *OlOk'*

Or+ /-ok'/= *OrOk'*

(iii) The initial vowel of /-ok'/ optionally becomes /u/ when it follows a root ending with c' (vide 4.3.6.1(i) :

gOc'+ /-ok'/ = *gujuk'*

Morphophonological changes before the stem suffixes.

(i) The final checked consonants of the roots become voiced when they are followed by /-ok'/

EhOp'+ /ok'/= *EhObOk'*

mak'+ /-ok'/= *magok'*

gOc'+ /-ok'/= *gojok'/gujak'*

(ii) The stem suffix optionally changes the quality of the root vowel in its own :

gOc'+ /-ok'/= *gojok'*

(iii) The final c′ of a root optionally changes the root vowel from o to u when /-ok′/ is added and the vowel of the suffix is also changed to u simultaneously (vide 4.3.6.1(i) :

gOc′ + /-ok′/ = *gujuk′*

Marker for The Active and Neutral

There are two sets of markers for the active and neutral stems — one set consisting of one member only i.e. /-t′/ for the active and the other set consisting of two members, i.e. /-ok′/ and /-n/ for the neutral.

The active marker is added to the tense/aspect markers when they are added to the active stems. The active marker is not added to the imperative with or without the aspect marker, to the invitative and subjunctive modal suffixes when they are added to the active stems.

The neutral marker /-ok′/ is added to all intransitive roots excepting a few like *topo* 'bathe', *ãRgo* 'descend' and *teṅgo/tiṅgu* 'stand', and optionally to the infixed (vide 4.3.3.1a) reciprocal stems when they are conjugated in simple present/future, present and past progressive and in the imperative mood, in other tenses /-n/ is added to the tense/aspect markers, to indicate the neutrality of the stems. In the subjunctive mood the neutral marker /-ok′/ is added, the modal suffix /-ke/ resulting in /-kok′/. The marker /-n/ is added to all other tense/aspect markers and to the imperative with the aspect suffix, to the invitative modal suffix when they are added to the neutral stems.

The three intransitive roots mentioned above (vide 4.4.3) take the neutral marker /-n/ instead of /-ok′/ when they are conjugated in the simple present/future, present and past progressive. In other tenses and moods /-n/ is suffixed to the tense/aspect and modal suffixes thus—

topo	'bathe'	*topon* 'id'
ãRgo	'descend'	*ãRgon* 'id'
teṅgo/tiṅgu	'stand'	*teṅgon/tiṅgun* 'id'

Aspect Suffixes

Santali employs a number of suffixes to denote different aspects. It is interesting to note that the suffixes which are employed to denote different states of action are also employed to express time dimension, thus, serving a dual role. Santali aspects may be broadly divided into non-completive and completive, both having two broad divisions — indeterminative and determinative. Non-completive indeterminative is indefinite while the same determinative is progressive. Completive indeterminative is aorist while the same determinative is either resultative stating an accomplished fact the result of which is still present or non-resultative stating an action which happened long ago and the result of which is no longer present or an action which is to be taken up prior to certain other action. In a tabular form they may be represented as follows :

Non-completive:

Indeterminative: indefinite - ϕ (zero)

Determinative : progressive - /-e/oo/kan

Completive :

Indeterminative: aorist - /-ke/-e/

Determinative : resultative - /-aka/

(accomplished and result is still present)

: non-resultative -

a. accomplished but result not obtained -/le/

b. priorative (action to be taken up prior to certain action) -/-le/

Non-completive determinative progressive is /-e/ in the active and /kan/ in the neutral. Indeterminative aorist in the completive is /-ke/ in the active and /-e/ in the neutral.

All the aspect suffixes except /ϕ/ and /kan/ are added with an active or neutral marker when they are suffixed to the respective stems. Thus, the aspect suffixes with the active and neutral markers are as follows—

Non-completive determinative progressive :

	Active	Neutral
	/-et'/	/kanϕ
Completive		
Indeterminative aorist	/-ket'/	/-en/
Determinative resultative	/-akat'/	/-akan/
non-resultative (accomplished)	/-let'/	/-len/
non-resultative (priorative)	/-le/	/-len/

Indeterminative aorist determinative non-resultative in the completive with the directional prefix /a-/ and with the benefactive stem suffix /-ka/ and the determinative resultative in the completive with direction /a-/ change their phonological shape. The changed forms are as follows—

Completive :

	Active	Neutral
Indeterminative aorist and determinative non-resultative		
(i) With the directional prefix	/-at'/	/an/
(ii) With the benefactive stem suffix	/-kat'/	
Completive :		
Determinative resultative with the directional prefix	/-aka-w- a-t'/	/-aka-w-a-n/

Morphophonological Changes

1. at'	*aet'	*aket'	a + ket'
2. at'	*aet'	*alet'	a + let'
3. an	*aen	*alen	a + len
4. an	*alen	a + len	
5. -kat	*kaet'	*kaket'	ka + ket'
6. -kat'	*kaet'	*kalet'	ka + let'
7. -akawat'		*aəkət'	aka + a + t'

Tense Markers

It is already noted that, in Santali, the aspect suffixes are employed to denote different time dimensions. Except the particles /kan/ and /tabEkan/or/tahEc'/ for the present and past respectively there are no separate tense markers. But the concept of time dimension in present, past and future is there and the different aspect suffixes along with their own functions denote different times.

The particle /kan/ denotes the present tense. It is quite different from other aspect-tense suffixes. While the aspect tense suffixes take object after them it takes the object before it, i.e. between the stem and /kan/. Again, it has nothing to do with active or neutral, therefore, it is used with both types of stems. It is also independently conjugated; thus—

kan-a-ñ	'I am'
kan-a-m	'you are'
kan-a-e	'he is'

It is secondarily shifted to the non-completive determinative progressive in the neutral and in the active with first and third person singular object. Example—

a. /kan/ as present tense marker :

uni dOhOR-(kan)-a-e	'he is a man'
nui hOR dOkhepa-(kan)-a-e	'this man is mad'

b. /kan/ as a non-completive determinative progressive marker:

uni calak'- (kan)-a-e	'he is going'
uni dal-iñ-(kan)-a-e	'he is beating me'

/tahEkan/ denotes the past tense and like /kan/ it is independently conjugated, as

tahẼkan-e-ñ	'I was'
tahẼkan-a-m	'you were'
tahẼkan-a-e	'he was'

The form is attested as such in the Northern dialect, while in the Southern dialect /tahEc'/ is attested, both having the same function. Example—

mit'Tan bir (tahẼkan)-a/(tahẼc')	'there was a forest'
unirEn oRak' gomke əDi napay(tahẼkan)-a- e/(tahẼc)-e	'his wife was very beautiful'

By the composition of /tahẼkan/ - /tahẼc'/ and different aspect suffixes different tense nuances are also indicated. The tense nuances expressed by this particle being used after the aspect suffixes will be shown in the aspect/tense network.

Zero or the absence of any marker denotes the future tense. However, the priorative aspect suffix may be used in the future giving the tense of anterior future.

The aspect-cum-tense network can be enumerated as follows—

Present tense :

Non-completive indeterminative indefinite as Simple Present --	φ (zero) active/ neutral)
Non-completive determinative progressive as Present Progressive - -	/et'/ (active) /kan/ (neutral)

Past tense :

Completive indeterminative aorist as Simple Past --	/-ket'/ (active) /-en/ (neutral)
Completive determinative resultative as Perfect --	/-akat'/ (active) /-akan/ (neutral)
Do with /tahEkan/ - /tahEc'/ as Past Perfect --	/-akat' tahẼkan/- /-akat' tahẼc'/ (active) /-akan tahẼkah/ - /-akan tahẼc'/ (neutral)
Completive determinative non-resultative (action not obtained) as as Plu-Perfect --	/-let'/ (active) /-len/ (neutral)
Do with /-tahEkan/ -- /tahEc'/ as Anterior Plu-Perfect --	/let' tahẼ/-/ -let 'tahẼc'/ (active) /-len tahẼkan/ -/-len taẼc'/ (neutral)
: Non-completive determinative progressive with /tahEkan/- /tahEc'/ as Past Progressive	/'tahẼkan/-et' tahẼc'/ (active) /kah tah Ẽkan/ - /kan tahEc'/(neutral)

Future tense :

Simple Future --	φ (Zero) (active)/(neutral)

Morphophonological Changes of the Suffixes

(i) The final t' of the suffixes becomes /-d-/ when a vowel follows:

dal + /-et'/ + /a/ + *e* = *daledae* 'he is beating'

dal + /-ket'/+/a/ + *e* = *dalkedae* 'he beat'

(ii) The final t' of the suffixes becomes /[*t'*]/ when a k follows:

dal + /-ket'/ + *kin* + /a/ + e = *dalket'kinae* 'he beat them (two)'

Example are illustrative of the use of different aspect- tense markers with two groups of stems, active and neutral. (The examples are given with hyphens in between the morphemes).

Simple Present

a. With active stems[5] :

Transitive root	*dal-e-a-e* beat-3po-fm-3ps	'he beats him'
	dal - a - e beat-fm-3ps	'he beats'
Transitive-intransitive root: (when the transitive meaning is prominent)	*gitic' - e - a - e* lay - 3po-fm-3ps	'he lays him'
Causative stem :	*dalocolhOcO - m - a - e* cause to beat -2ps-fm-3ps	'he causes you to beat'
Permissive stem:	*ñElocolhOcO - ñ a-e* allow to see-1po-fm-3ps	'he lets/me to see'
Benefactive stem :	*tOlkak' -a - e* bind for someone-fm-3ps	'he binds it (for somebody)'
	tOlka - e - a - e bind for some-one-3ps-fm-3ps	'he binds (the cow) (do)
Compound stem of two : transitive roots	*sendrañam - e - a - e* seek and find -3po-fm-3ps	'he searches and finds him'
	sendrañam - a - e + seek and find -fm-3ps	'he searches and finds'

Compound stem in which: the last component is transitive	*sEndore - a - e* able to go-fm-3ps	'he is able to go'

b. With the neutral stems :

Intransitive roots :	*sEnOk' - a - e* go - fm-3ps	'he goes'
Transitive - intransitive root (when the intransitive meaning is prominent)	*giric' - a - e* lie-fm - 3ps	'he lies'
Reciprocal stem :	1. *dapal - a - kin* beat each -fm-3ps (dl)	'The (two) beat each other'
	2. *dalok' - a - kin*	'id'
Passive stem :	*dalok' - a - e* be beaten - fm-3po	'he is beaten'
Reflexive stem :	*ñElok' - a - e* see oneself-fm-3ps	'he sees himself'
Mediopassive stem :	*daljOṅ - a - e* beat for oneself-fm-3ps	'he beats (thrashes) for himself'
Compound of two intransitive roots	*rakap' hijuk'-a-e* ascend and come-fm-3ps	'he ascends and comes'

PRESENT PROGRESSIVE

a. With Active stems :

Transitive roots :	*dal-ed-a-e* beat-prP-fm-3ps	'he is beating'
	dal - e - kan - a - e beat - 3ps-Prp-fm-3ps	'he is beating him'
	dal - ed - e - a - e beat -prp-3po-fm-3ps	'he is beating him'

Transitive-intransitive roots in which the transitive meaning is prominent

1. *gOc' - ed - a - e* 'he is killing'
kill - prp - fm - 3ps
2. *gOc' - et' - e-a - e* 'he is killing him'
kill - prp-3po-fm-3ps
gOc' - e - kan - a - e 'id'
prp

Causative stem :
daloco/hOcO - et' - me-a-e 'he is causing you to beat'
cause to beat - prp
-2po-fm-3ps
daloco/hOcO-e - kan - a - e 'he is causing him to beat'
daloco/hOcO - ed - e - a - e 'id'.

Permissive stem :
ñEloco/hOcO-a - e - kan - a - e 'he is allowing him to see'
allow to
see-dt-3po-prp-fm-3ps

Benefactive stem :
tOlkak' - kan-a-e 'he is binding (for somebody)'
bind for
someone-prp-fm-3ps
tOlka - e - kan - a - e 'he is binding it (cow) (for somebody)'
-3po-prp-fm-3ps

Compound of two transitive roots :
mak'ǝgu-ed- a-e 'he is outting and bringing'
out and bring-prp-fm-3ps

Compound stem in which :
the second component is a
transitive root
sEndare - e - a - e 'he is able to go'
able to go prp- fm-3ps

b. With neutral stem :
Intransitive root : *sEnOk' - kan - a - e* 'he is going'
go - Prp - fm - 3ps

Transitive-intransitive (when the intransitive meaning is prominent) *gujuk' - kan - a - e* 'he is dying'
die - Prp-fm-3ps

Reciprocal stem :

1. *dapal - kan - a - kin* — They are beating each other'
   beat each other
   -Prp-fm-3ps(dl)
2. *dalok' - kan - a - kin* — 'id'

Passive stem : *dalok' - kan - a- e* — 'he is being beaten'
be beaten -Prp-fm-3ps

Reflexive stem : *nElOK' - kan - a - e* — 'he is seeing himself'
see oneself - Prp-fm-3ps

Mediopassive : *daljOn̈ - kan - a - e* — 'he is beating for himself'
beat for oneself -prp-fm-3ps

Compound stem of :
ruəRhijuk' - kan - a - e — 'he is returning coming back'
return and come-Prp-fm-3ps
two intransitive roots

SIMPLE PAST

a. With Active stems :

Transitive root : *dal - ked - a - e* — 'he beat'
beat - p - fm - 3ps
dal-led-e-a-e — 'he beat him'
beat-P-3po-fm-3ps

Do with dative (indirect object) *ləi - at' -ko-a - e* — 'he told them'
tell- 3po-fm-3ps

Transitive-intransitive root (when the transitive meaning is prominent *gOc' -ked - a - e* — 'he killed'
kill -P -fm - 3ps
gOc' - ked e - a - e — 'he killed him'
kill-P - 3po-fm-3ps

Causative stem : *daloco/hOcO - ked-e-a-e* 'he caused him to beat'
cause to beat -P-3po-fm-3ps
hEc'oco/hOcO -ked-e-a-ko 'they caused him to come'
cause to come-P-3po-fm-3ps(pl)

Permissive stem: *gOc'oco/hOcO -ad-e-a-lE* 'we let him die'
allow to die-dir.& p-3po-fm-lps(pl)

hEc'oco/hOcO -ad-e-a-ko 'they permitted him to come'
allow to come-dir.& P-3po-fm-3ps(pl)

ñEloco/hOcO -ad-e-a-e 'he permitted him to see'
allow to see - dir. & P-3po-fm-3ps

Benefactive stem :

dapalked - a - e 'they covered (for someone)'
cover for & p -fm-3po someone

uyuk'kad - e - a - e 'he covered it (cow) (to
cover for someone & P help someone)'

Compound of two :
transitive *ñElñam* - ked - a - e 'he saw and found'
roots see and find -p - fm-3ps

Compound in which the second component is a transitive root

sEndare - ed - a - e 'he was able to go'
able to go -dir & p-fm-3ps

b. With neutral stems :

Intransitive root : *sEn - en - a - e* 'he went'
go -p - fm - 3ps

Transitive-intransitive root when the intransitive meaning is
prominent *gOc' en - a - e* 'he died'
die - p - fm-3ps

Reciprocal stem: 1. *depal -en - a - kin* 'they (two) beat each
beat each other other'
-P-fm-3ps(dl)

2. *dal -en - a - kin*

Passive stem : *dal -en - a - e* 'he was beaten'
beat -P -fm-3ps

Do of causative: *gOc'oco/hOcO -en - a - e* 'he was caused to die'
cause to die -p-fm-3ps

Reflexive stem : *ñEl - en - a - e* 'he saw himself'
see -p-fm - 3ps

Mediopassive stem :*dal - an - a - e* 'he beat/thrashed for himself'

Compound of two :		
intransitive roots	*ruəRhEc' - en - a - e*	'he come back'
	return & come-p-fm-3ps	

Perfect

a. With Active stems :

Transitive root :	*dal - akad - a - e*	'he has beaten him'
	beat - perf - fm-3ps	
	dal - akad - e - a -e	'he has beaten him'
	beat -perf-3ps-fm-3ps	
Do with dative :	*ləi - akawad-e-a-e*	he has told him'
/a - /	tell -peff & dir-3po-fm-3ps	
Transitive-intransitive root (when the transitive meaning is		
prominent	*gOc' - akad - a - e*	'he has killed'
	kill -perf -fm-3ps	
Causitive :	*daloco/hOcO -akad-e-a-e*	'he has caused him
	cause to beat -perf-3po-fm-3ps	to beat'
Permissive :	*daloco/hOcO - akawad-e-a-e*	'he has permitted
	allow to beat -perf & dt-3po-fm-3ps	him to beat'
	gOc'oco/hOcO -akawad-e-a-e	'he has let him die'
	allow to die-Perf & dt-3po-fm-3ps	
Benefactive	--	
Compound of two :	*mak'əgu-akad-a-e*	'he has cut and brought'
transitive roots	cut and bring-Perf-fm-3ps	
Compound in which :	*sEndare-akawad-a-e*	'he has been able to go'
the second component	able to go-Perf & dir.-fm-3ps	
is a transitive root		

b. With neutral stems :

Intransitive root :	*sEn-akan-a-e*	'he has gone'
Transitive-intransitive	go-Perf-fm-3ps	
root (when the	*gOc' - akan - a - e*	'he has died'
intransitive meaning	die-perf-fm-3ps	
is prominent)		

Reciprocal : 1. *dapal-akan-a-kin* 'they (two) have
beat each other- beaten each other'
perf-fm-3ps(dl)
2. *dal-akan-a-kin*

Passive : *dal -akan - a - e* 'he has been beaten'
beat-perf-fm-3ps

Do of causative *gOc'oco/hOcO-akan-a-e* 'he has been caused
cause to die-perf-fm-3ps to die'

Reflexive : *ñEl-akan-a-e* 'he has seen himself'
see - perf-fm-3ps

Mediopassive : *dal -akawan-a-e* 'he has beaten (padd)
beat-perf-& dir-fm-3ps for himself'

Compound of two: *ruəRhEc' - akan - a - e* 'he has come back'
intransitive roots return and come-perf-fm-3ps

Pluperfect

a. With Active stems :

Transitive root : *dal - led -a - e* 'he had beaten'
beat -plu.perf -fm-3ps
dal -led -e -a -e 'he had beaten him'
-3po-

Transitive-intransitive root (when the transitive meaning is
prominent) *gOc' -led a - e* 'he had killed'
Kill
gOc' -led - e - a - e 'he had killed him'
-3po-

Causative : *daloco/hOcO -led-e-a-e* 'he had cause him to beat'
cause to beat

Permissive : *daloco/hOcO-ad-e-a-e* 'he had permitted
pillow to beat -dt & plu.perf him to beat'

Benefactive : *pOtOmkad - a - e* 'he had covered
cover (for someone) & plu.perf (for someone)

Compound of two: *mak'əgu -led - a - e* 'he had cut and brought'
transitive roots cut and bring

Compound in which the second component is a transitive root : *sEndare - ad - a - e* 'he had been able to go' able to go-dir & plu.perf

---

b. With Neutral stems :

Intransitive root : *sen - len - a - e* 'he had gone'
go -plu perf -fm-3ps

Transitive-intransitive root (when the intransitive is prominent) *gOc' - len - a - e* 'he had died'
die - plu perf - fm-3ps

Reciprocal : 1. *dapal - len - a - kin* 'they had beaten each other'
beat each other - plu perf - fm - Bps (dl)

2. *dal-len-a-kin* 'they had beaten each other'

Passive : *dal-len-a-e* 'he had been beaten'
-3ps

Reflexive : *ñEl-len-a-e* 'he had seen himself'
see perf & refl - fm-3ps

Mediopassive : *ñEl-an-a-e* 'he had seen for himself'
see-dt & plu perf -fm-3ps

Compound of two : *ãRgohEc'-len-a-e* 'he had descended and come'
descend and come

Anterior Pluperfect

---

a. With the Active stems :

Transitive roots : *idi-let'-ko-tahẼkan-a-ko* 'they had taken them away'
take away-plu perf-3po (pl)-fm-3ps (pl)

Do with dative /a/ : *lɘi-ad-iñ- tahẼkana-e* 'he had told me'
lell-dt & plu perf-lps-p-fm-3ps

Transitive-intransitive: *gOc'-let'-ko-tahẼkan-a-e* he had killed then' root (when the transitive meaning is prominent)

Causative:	*daloco/hOcO-let'-kin-tahẼkan-a-e* cause to beat	'he had caused them (two) to beat'
Permissive:	*ñEloco/hOcO-ad-e-tahẼhan-a- ko* allow to see	'they had permitted him to see'
Benefactive :	*dapalkad-e-tahEkan-a-e* cover for someone & plu perf	'he had covered it (axim) for someone'
Compound of : two transitive see and find roots	*ñElñam-led-e-tahEkan-a-e* -plu perf-eps-P-fm-3ps	'he had seen and found him'
Compound in which : the second component is a transitive root.	*sEndare-at'-tahẼkan-a-e* able to go-dt & plu perf-P-fm-3ps	'he had been able to go'

b. With the neutral stems :

Intransitive root :	*hEc'-len-tahẼkan-a- ñ* come-plu perf-p-fm-lps	'I had come'
Transitive-intransitive root (when the transitive meaning is prominent) die	*gOc'-len-tahẼkan-a-e* die-p-p-fm-3ps	'he had died'
Reciprocal :	1. *dapal-len-tahẼkan-a-kin* beat each other	'id'
Passive :	*ñam-len-tahEkan-a-kin* find -3ps	'it had been found'
Reflexive :	*ñEl-len-tahẼkan-a-e* see -3ps	'he had seen himself'
Mediopassive :	*dal-an-tahẼkan-a-e* beat-dt & plu perf-P-fm-dps	'he had beaten (paddy) for himself'
Compound of two intransitive root:	*ãRgo hEc' - len- tahEkan-a-e*	'he had descended and come'

Past Progressive

a. With Active stems :

Transitive root :	*dal-et'-tahẼkan-a-e* beat-p-p-fm-3ps	'he was beating'
	dal-et'-me-tahẼkan-a-e	'he was beating you'
Transitive-intransitive root (when the transitive meaning is prominent)	*bancao -et'-ko-tahẼkan-a-e* save	'he was saving them'
Causative :	*daloco/hOcO-ed-e-tahẼkan-a-e* cause to beat	'he was causing him to beat'
Permissive :	*ñEloco/hOcO-a-e-kin-tahẼkan-a- e* allow to see-dt-3ps-p-p-fm-3ps	'he was permitting him to see'
Benefactive :	*tOlka-a-kan-tahẼkan-a-e* bind for someone -3ps-p-p-fm-3ps	'he was binding it (cow) for someone'
Compound of : two transitive roots	*mak 'əgu-et'-tahẼkan-a- e* cut and bring	'he was cutting and bringing'
Compound in : which the second component is a transitive root.	*sEndare-et'-tahẼkan-a-e* able to go	'he waş being able to go'

b. With Neutral stems :

Intransitive root :	*sEnOk'-kan-tahẼkan-a-e-* go -p - p -fm-3ps	'he was going'
Transitive-intran- : sitive root (when the intransitive meaning is prominent)	*gujuk'-kan-tahẼkan-a-e* die -p -p -fm-3ps	'he was going'
Reciprocal :	1. *dapal-kan-tahẼkan-a-kin* beat each other	'they (two) were beating each other'

	2. *dalok'-kan-tahẼkan-a-kin* beat each other	'id'
Passive :	*ñamok'-kan-tahẼkan-a* be found -3ps	'it was being found'
Reflexive :	*ñElOk'-kan-tahẼkan-a-e* see oneself -3ps	'he was seeing himself'
Mediopassive :	*doljOṅ-kaṇ-tahẼkan-a-e* beat for oneself	'he was beating for himself'
Compound of two intransitive roots :	*ruərhijuk'-kan-tahẼkan-a-e* return and come	'he was returning'

Simple Future

Same as Simple Present

Here, in the examples of the causative, permissive, the stem suffix of both the dialects are given separated, by a dash, the first stem suffix /-oco/ belongs to the northern dialect and /- hOcO/ to the Southern. The alternative /tahẼc'/ in the Southern dialect as the past indicator in the past progressive is also indicated in the table.

Mood

The action or events in Santali can be divided as real (indicative), as desired (optative) or simply as possible (subjunctive) as needed or advisable (imperative) and as welcoming (invitative). The mood for the optative and the subjunctive can be subsumed under subjunctive since the marker is the same for both and the various meanings are often fluid and vague and in many respects almost indentical.

There is no special marker for the prohibitive mood, the prohibitive particle /alo/ being used before the verb in the simple present / future expresses prohibition which can better be termed negative imperative (a sort of 'don't'), although the finite /a/ is used at the end of the verb which is understood in the imperative.

Example —

alo-m calak' - a	'do not go'
alo -pE rOR - a	'do not speak'
alo - mdal - e - a	'do not beat him'
ñut - rE alo - m dəRbaRay - a	'do not run about in the dark'

There is no special marker for the conditional mood. The conditional particle / khan / with or without the priorative aspect suffix /-le/-len/ denotes conditionality. Example —

janwar-iñ ñam - le - ko - khan əgu-ko-a-ñ 'if I find them (animals) I shall bring them'

ba-ñ sEn-len -khan uni ba-e hijuk'-a 'if I do not go he will not come'

Indicative : ϕ (zero). It indicates the reality of an action and the normal verb in different tenses serves the purpose of an indicative mood.

Subjunctive : /ke / active.
/kok' / neutral.

It is formed by adding /-ke/ to the active stems and /-kok'/ to the neutral and indicated the desire or an action on the part of the subject or simple possibility of an action. The modal suffix takes the object infix after it. The different forms of /- ke/ with the object infix are tabulated below —

Person		Number		
		Singular	Dual	Plural
First	Inclusive	-kiñ	-kelaṅ -	kebon
	Exclusive		-keliñ	-kelE
Second		-kem	-keben(N.S.) -kebin (S.S.)	-kepa
Third		-ke	-kikin	-keko

Example —
Active :

uni dal - (kiñ) -a-e 'he might beat me'

onko/unku iñ kichu - ko Em-(kiñ)-a 'they might give me something'

mig'Takam Em - (kiñ)-a 'would you give me one rupee'.

unkon Daṅra -m əkhriñ- (kikin) a 'would you be willing to sell'

Thik dam-iñ ñam-le-khan əkhriñ(kekin)-a-ñ 'if I get proper price I might sell them'

ranoco/hOcO-(ke)-a-ñ 'had I been able to cause him to treat medically'

unkin orka'-rE idid-(kikin)-a 'had I been able to take them (two) home'

Daṅra-koOhO-ñ əkhriñ-(keko)-a 'I would never sell the cows'

Neutral :

calao-(kok')-a-ñ 'I might go'

gidrə ba-ñ bancao-le-khan gOc'-(kok')-a- e 'if I had not saved the child he might have died'

ba-ñ sEn-len-khan ba-ñ ñapam-(kok')-a 'if I do not go I might not meet'

ba-m sEn-len-khan iñ hõba-ñ sEn-(kok')-a 'if you do not go I also might not go'

noa-m Em-kok'-a 'would you like to give this ?

be-m hOhO-iñ-khan kharañ-rE- ñ ñur-(kok')-a 'had you not called me I might have fallen in the ditch'

tapam-(kok')-a-kin 'they might have fought each other'

ojha-ThEn-iñ ranoco/hOcO- (kok')-a 'had I been treated by the Ojha'

Morphophonological Changes :

(i) The final vowel of /-ke/ elided before another vowel of the neutral marker and the object infix; thus

ke + -ok' = kok'

ke + e(3rd person sg. object) = ke

(ii) The final vowel of /-ke/ becomes high /i/ before the first person sg. and third person dual suffixes (vide 4.7.3.1) :

dal-kiñ-a-e 'he might beat me'

əkhariñ-kikin-a-m 'would you be willing to sell these two ?'

Imperative :

There is no separate marker for the imperative. It is formed by adding /-mE/, /-ben/ (N.S.) or /-bin/ (S.S.) and /-pE/ for the 2nd person singular, dual and plural respectively either to the active or neutral stem directly or to the priorative aspect /-le/ (active). /-len/ (neutral) which follows the stem or to the object infix if there is any. The finite marker /a/ is not used.

Example —
Active —

uni met-a-e-(mE)	'tell him'
ləi-(mE)	*'tell'*
EsEt'kak'-(mE)	'cover (it) for someone'

godrə dOhOka-e-(mE)	'keep the child'
daloco / hOcO-e-(m)	'cause him to beat'
ñEloco/hOcO-a-ko-(mE)	'let him see'
sEnOco/hOcO -a-ko-(mE)	'let him go'
gidrə gitic'-e-(m)	'lay the child'
pERa Em-le-ko-(pE)	'give friends first'
jOmak' jOm-le-(m)	'eat food first'
lahatE jOm-le-(m) adO-ñ calak'-a	'eat first, then I go'
lahatE Em-le-(m) adO-ñ mEn-a	'give first, then I will say'
Neutral :	
cãRtE hijuk-(mE)	'come quickly'
ma duRup'-(mE)	'please sit down'
gitic'-(mE)	'lie down'
ñElok-mE	'see yourself'
dare-khOn argon-(pE)	'descend from the tree'
noa-khOn bacaojOṅ-(mE)	'take from this'
rakap'hijuk'-(mE)	descend and come from the tree'
ranocok'-(ben)	'be medically treated (N.S.)
ranhOcOk'-(bin)	'id' (S.S.)
laha-tE calao-len-(mE) adOm ləi-a	'go first, then you will say',

Morphophonoligical Change

The second person singular /-mE/ optionally become /-m/ after vowel of the objective infix but not the rule after the priorative aspect suffix /-le/ and benefactive stem suffix /-ka/ it is the rule, like

ma duRup'-ko-(m)	'please make them sit'
Em-a-ko-(m)	'give them'
maraṅ hatao-le-(m)	'take first'
dapalka-(m)	'cover it (for someone)'
but DanratOlka-e-(mE)	*'bind the cow (to help someone)'*
calaooco-a-ko-(mE)	'let him go'

Invitative :

/-le/ active

/-len/ neutral

The invitative mood is formed by adding /-le/ and /-len/ along with the emphatic particle go to the active and neutral stems respectively. The contracted forms of the first person inclusive dual *lan* and plural *bon* follow the emphatic /ge/ if the invitative particle *dEla* is not used before the verb, but if it is so used *lan* and *bon* are added to it. The finite marker /a/ is not used.

Example —

dEla-bon jOm-(le)-ge or *jOm-(le)-ge-bon* 'come, let us eat'

dEla-bon sap'-(le)-ge *sap'-(le) ge-bon* 'come, let us catch it'

dEla-bon sap'-(le)-ge *rəput'- (le)-ge-laṅ* 'come, let us break it'

dEla-laṅ 'sap'-(le)-ge/ sap '-(le)-ge- laṅ 'come, let us swim'

dEla-bon payra-(len)-ge/payra-(len)-ge-bon 'come, let us swim'

dEla-laṅ tahẼ - (len)-ge/ tahẼ-(len)-ge-laṅ 'come, let us stay'

Morphophonological Changes :

(i) The final vowel of /le/ is elided before the 3rd person singular object infix, i.e. /-le/ + e = le, as in

uni sap'-le-ge-laṅ 'come, let us catch him'

Pronominal Incorporation :

The incorporation of the animate subject or object in the verb phrase in the short form of the personal pronouns (except in ('I') is obligatory in Santali. When the subject or object of a sentence is a personal pronoun it is shown in the verb phrase by its contracted form. When an animate noun fills the subject or object slot of a sentence the contracted form of the 3rd personal pronoun is used in the verb phrase. The contracted form of the pronoun for the animate subject may be suffixed to the finite marker /a/ or to the word preceding the verb. The animate object is always infixed within the verb. The infix for the indirect object, always takes a dative marker /a/ which is either attached to it as in simple present-future and present and past progressive or incorporated within the aspect/tense suffixes. Unlike indirect object there is no special marker for the direct object, the infixed contracted forms of the personal pronouns express it.

Parallel to the independent personal pronouns the incorporated forms are also eleven in number, in a tabular form they can be represented thus—

		Number		
Person		Singular	Dual	Plural
First	Inclusive		*lań*	*bon/bo*
	Exclusive			
		ñ	*liñ*	*lE*
Second		m -mE -me	*ben/bin*	*pE*
Third		*e*	*kin*	*ko*

All these contracted forms (except-mE and -ml-) are used as suffixes or infixes, so the suffix and infix signs are avoided. In the second person dual the two forms *ben* and *bin* represent the Northern and Southern dialect respectively. The form /-me-/ in the second person singular is specifically used as the object infix, the form *m* is used as the subject suffix, indirect object infix with dative /a-/. The form /mE/ in the second person singular is specifically used as the imparative suffix. The contracted form for the first person plural inclusive is *bon* while the independent form is *abo,* although the contracted form *bo* is sporadically attested in the Southern dialect.

Morphophonological Changes

(i) *m,* as suffix, gets an increment e in the initial position when it is added to a word ending in a consonant', *iskul-em calak'-a* 'do you go to school ?'

(ii) The third person singular e as suffix becomes i after words ending in /i/ /u/ /a/ and forms a diphthong with it and becomes semivocalic :

uni gidra-i gitic' hOcO-e-kan-a 'he is causing the child to lie'

uni-i calak'-a 'he will go'

unku-i met-a-ko-a 'he told them'

(iii) The third person singular e suffix or infix when added to a word ending in /a/ or / / forms a diphthong with it and becomes semivocalic : as

uni calak'-á-e 'hẹ goes, will go'

gidra doh ka-e-m 'keep the child'

(iv) The first person singular suffix gets an increment /i / when occurs after a root or suffix ending in a consonent :

dal-akad-in-a-e 'he has beaten me

The pronominal genitive may be infixed within the verb to represent the possessor and in that case the contracted forms of the personal pronouns except in take the prefix /ta-/. The possessive infixes can be tabulated as follows —

Person		Number: Singular	Dual	Plural
First	Inclusive Exclusive	-tiñ -taliñ-	-talaṅ- -talE-	- tabon-
Second		-tam-	-taben- /-tabin	-tapE-
Third		-tae-	-takin-	-tako-

Examples —

(S.S.) *cet'jinis henak'-tabin-a* 'which thing are there of you' ?

(S.S.) *uni-ic' ∂Diuste gidr∂ko tanẼkan-tae-a* 'there are many sons of him'

(N.S.) *unkin-rEn mit 'ṬEc' kora gidr∂-e tahẼkan-takin-a* 'they had one male child'

Morphophonological Change

The final vowel of the prefix /ta-/ is elided before in, as in /ta/ + in /tiñ/

Marker for the finite verb /a/: The finite verbs in Santali are always suffixed by /a/. This /a/ gives the sentence a 'demonstrated reality'. This is attached to all aspect / tenses and moods except the imperative and the invitative. In the protasis portion of a conditional clause it is not added. It is generally suffixed at the end of the verb provided the pronominal subject is suffixed to the word preceding the verb. But if it is not added to the preceding word this /a/ is prefinal i.e. the subject pronoun comes after it. Example —

hana oRak'-rE loTa menak'-a 'there is pot in that house'

uni ato-rE-e calak'kan-a	'he is going to the village'
alom ORhẼ-iñ-a	'do not sing in my praise'
mit' ghəRic' tahEn-mE	'stay for a while'
dEla-bon sEn-len-ge	'come, let us go'
ba-m hOhO-iñ-khan ñur-kok'-a-ñ	'if you did not call me I might have fallen in the ditch'

Dative marker /at'/ : Santali possesses a dative marker /a/ which marks the indirect object or the dative case. In the active stems it takes the object after this. In the neutral it is used in the medio-passive stem to indicate the subject who is logically the indirect object. In certain cases however, as in the simple past and plu. perfect it is prefixed to the aspect/tense markers, as in

a + ket' (simple past) = at'

a + let' (plu. perfect) = at'

But in certain cases as in the perfect it is added to the aspect/tense in such a way as would give it an infixal character, as in

aka + w + a + t' = akawat'

aka + w + a + n' = akawan'

Total inventory of the verbal formatives : Santali verbal formative elements can be divided into five groups - primary (stem formatives), secondary (aspect/tense and modal formatives), tertiary (active, neutral, dative and possessive (formatives), quarternary (personal markers), and finite. All the formatives are listed below:

(i) Primary :

Causative / permissive	:	a-; -oco (N.S.); - hOcO(S.S.)
Reciprocal	:	-p-; -ok' (N.S. only)
Benefactive	:	-ka
Passive/Reflexive	:	-ok'
Mediopassive	:	-jOṅ
Iterative/Intensive	:	Reduplication

(ii) Secondary :

Simple present / future :		
Present progressive	:	-a (active) (particle) kan (particle) (neutral) used to denote present also.

	Simple past	:	-ke (active)
			-e (neutral)
	Perfect	:	-aka
	Pluperfect	:	-le
	Past	:	tehEkan (particle)
	Indicative mood	:	ϕ (zero)
	Subjanctive mood	:	-ke (active)
			-kok' (neutral)
	Invitative mood	:	le + ge (particle)
(iii)	Tertiary:		
	Active	:	-t'
	Neutral	:	-n; -ok'
	Dative	:	a-
	Possessive	:	ta-

(iv) Quarternary :

Pronominal suffixes and infixes : iñ, -ñ, laṅ, liñ, bon, lE, m, -mE, -me, ben (N.S.), bin (S.S.), pE, e, kin, ko.

(v) Finite verb marker : -a.

Regarding the entry of certain formatives under primary or tertiary and the listing certain points need mentioning. Within the lists the dialectal variations like /-oco/ in the Northern and /-hOcO/ in the Southern dialect as causative formative, /ben/ in the Northern dialect and /bin/ in the Southern dialect as 2nd person dual subject or object marker, /-ok'/ among the teenager in the Northern dialect as reciprocal formative, are entered and this is done to represent a clearer picture.

Only the particle for the past /tahẼc' / in the Southern dialect is not entered in the list. In the Southern dialect /tahẼkan/ as the past indicator retain its form, only in the past progressive it becomes /tahẼc'/.

Pinnow[6] (1966); has mentioned /-ok'/ and /-jOṅ/ as the tertiary suffixes. But here in contradiction to Pinnow, /-ok'/ is entered under both primary and tertiary affixes and /-jOṅ/ under primary affixes. The reason behind their entry under the primary affixes is that they are taking the place of the primary affixes i.e.

they are attached to the root and modify its meaning in forming stems like passive, reflexive, mediopassive and sometimes also reciprocal, though they are not conjugated throughout all tenses and are replaced by certain other affixes. But it is true that in modifying the meaning of the roots they are playing an important role. /-ok'/ also enters in the list as the tertiary suffix, as then it is added either to the stems already formed or to the subjective suffix and there it indicates neutrality.

Non-finite Verb

Gerund : The gerund is formed by adding /katE/ to the verb stems active or neutral :

dalkatE	'having beaten'
kəmikatE	'having done'
jOmkatE	'having eaten'
dalok'katE	'having been beaten'
tiəoco/hOcO katE	'having caused to bring down'
ñEljOṅkatE	'having seen for ownself'
sEnkatE '	having gone'

References

1. There is a strong tendency among the speakers in the Southern dialect and also among the youngsters in the Northern dialect to eliminate the finite marker in the past-progressive although the action concerned is finite.
2. 'Another way is to infix a /-k'-/ after the initial or first vowel ... This may be done with all base words' - P.O. Bodding, Materials For A Santali Grammar (Dumka, 1929), p. 168.
3. (N.S.) Stands for Northern Santali.
4. (S.S.) Stands for Southern Santali.
5. Abbreviations will fead as
   1_p = first person pro = present
   2_p = second person p = progressive
   3_p = third person perf = perfect p = past
   o = object refl = reflexive
   s = subject
   dt = dative
   fm = finite marker.
6. H.J. Pinnow, 'A Comparative study of the verb in the Munda languages' In : Zide(ed) Studies in Comparative Austroasiatic Linguistics. The Hague : Mouton, pp.96, 103.

5

ADJECTIVE & NUMERAL

1. Adjective

The root morphemes, derivative morphemes and the phrases which serve as attributes in endocentric attributive constructions and as pridicate complements in subject-predicate complement sentences are grouped as adjective in Santali. The adjectives, in Santali, do not agree in number or in gender except in a few borrowed items, and in case with their qualified nouns. Some examples are —

a. As attributes in endocentric attributive construction :

jhOtOm koRako 'all boys', *jhOtOm* 'all', attribute, *koRako* 'boys; head.

marań bin 'big snake', *marań* 'big', attribute, *bin* 'snake', head.

bis lədu 'poisonous sweet', *bis* 'poisonous', attribute, *lədu* 'sweet', head.

onkan katha 'word like that', *onkan* 'like that', attribute, *katha* 'word', head.

jãhãn kami 'any work', *jãhãn* 'any', attribute, *kəmi* 'work', head.

daraykan serma 'coming year', *daraykan* 'coming', attribute, *serma* 'year', head.

oRak'rEn hOR man belonging to the house', *oRak'rEn* 'belonging to the house', attribute, *hOR* 'man' head.

b. **As predicate complement :**

uni dO kala-ge-a-e 'he is deaf; *kala* 'deaf' predicate complement.

nui dO koṅka-ge-a-e 'this one is mad', *koṅka* 'mad', predicate complement.

phulmoni dO kuṅki-ge-a-e 'phulmani is mad', *kunki* 'mad', predicate complement.

koRa dO usul-ge-a-e 'the youth is tall', *usul* 'tall', predicate complement.

ona churi dO thubru-thobro-ge[1]*-a* 'that knife is blunt',

thubru~thobro 'blunt', predicate complement.

noa dO sebel~sibil-a 'this is palatable', *sebel~sibil* 'palatable', predicate complement.

nui gidrə dO bəric'-ge-a-e 'this child is bad', *baric'* 'bad', predicate complement.

uni dO kãRa-ge-a-e 'he is blind' *kãRa* 'blind', predicate complement.

uni dO kəRi-ge-a-e 'she is blind', *kãRi* 'blind', predicate complement.

tEṅgOc' dO ədi laser-a 'the axe (small) is very sharp', *laser* 'sharp', predicate complement.

seta dO khEpa-kan-a-e 'the dog is mad', *khEpa* 'mad', predicate complement.

budhiic' hOpOn khEpa-tahẼkan-a-e / tahẼc'-e 'the son of the old lady was mad'

The adjectives as predicate complements sometimes occur with the particle /ge/ but that is not the rule i.e. they may occur as such without the particle. In the subject-predicate complement sentences the adjectives are followed by the finite marker /a/ and occasionally by the particles /kan/ and /tahEkan/ for the present and past tenses respectively.

In a phrase having two layers of endocentric attributive constructions, an adjective may occur as the head of the first layer but ultimately the head of the whole construction is a noun. For example -

əDi maraṅ bin 'very big snake' has two layers -

əDi maraṅ 'very big' and *əDi maraṅ bin'* very big snake'.

In the first layer i.e. *əDi maraṅ, maraṅ* is the head which is modified by *ədi* 'very', but in the ultimate layer *bin* is the head attributed by *ədi maraṅ*.

Formation of adjectives :

On the formal criteria adjectives may be divided into four groups—simple, derivative, verbal and phrasal. Besides these, certain nouns and verbs are also used as adjectives in endocentric attributive constructions. Example —

lel utu 'meat curry', *jel* 'meat' and *utu* 'curry'
sendra koRa 'hunting boy', *sendra* 'hunt', *koRa* 'boy';
koRa gidrə 'male child', *koRa* 'boy', 'youngmen',
gidrə 'child'

Simple adjectives :

These are the root morphemes having the original adjectival value and which are obviously — simple and indecomposable and are used as attributes in endocentric attributive constructions and as predicate complements in subject-predicate complement sentences ; example —

a. Adjective	As Attribute
bhage 'good'	*bhage lədu* 'good sweet'
boge 'good'	*boge kuRi* 'good girl'
hEndE 'black'	*hEndE gəi* 'black cow'
arak' 'red'	*arak' rimil* 'red cloud'
ponD/põR 'white'	*ponD/põR bhit* 'white wall'
bele-bill ripe	*bele-bili ul* 'ripe mango'
Tuər 'orphan'	*tuər kuRi* 'orphan girl, young lady'
usul 'high'	*usul dOn* 'high jump'
jeleñ 'long'	*jeleñ dOn* 'long jump'

səri 'true, honest'	*səri hRr* 'honest man'
	səri katha 'true statement'
bəric' 'bad, wicked'	*bəric haRam* 'bad, wicked old man'
napay 'nice'	*napay tiriə* 'nice flute'
ləTu 'big'	*lətu gEDE* 'big duck'
rimsic' 'small'	*rimsic'jo* 'small fruit'

b. As predicate complement :

nui gəi dO hEndE-kan-a-e ~hEndE-ge-a-e ~hEndE-a- e 'this cow is black'

bhit dO ponO/põR-ge-a	'the wall is white'
nui dO rimsic'-ge-a-e	'he/she is small'
nui dO əDi bəric' -ge-a	'this person is very bad'
uniak' tiriə dO əDi napay-a	'his flute is very nice'

Derivative adjectives :

The adjectives which are derived from nouns, pronouns and pronominal adverbs by adding different suffixes are grouped as derivative adjectives. (for details of adjective derivation vide Ch. II) Like simple adjectives the derivative adjectives are also used as attributes in endocontric attributive constructions and as predicate complements.

Examples —

a. As attribute :

bOrOran gam 'fearful story', *bOtOran* 'fearful', attribute and *gam* 'story', head.

dayavan hOR 'kind man', *dayavan* 'kind', attribute and *hOR* 'man', head.

darean hOR 'strong man', *darean* 'strong' attribute and *hOR* man', head.

sakaman dare 'leaf-having tree', *sakaman* 'leaf having, attribute and *dare* 'tree' head.

hErElan Era 'husband-having lady', *hErElan* 'husband-having, attribute and *Era* 'lady', head.

jãhãn dOrkar 'any need', *jãhãn* 'any', attribute and *dOrkar* 'need', head.

noṅkan kəmi 'work like this', *noṅkan* 'like this', attribute and *kəmi* 'work', head.

noṅkan hOR 'man like this', *noṅkan* 'like this', attribute and *hOR* 'man', head.

okatEn gəDi 'car destined for where', *okatEn* 'destined for where', attribute and *gəDi* 'car', head.

okarEn goDet' 'messenger of where', *okarEn* 'of where', attribute and *goDet'* 'messenger', head.

b. As predicate complement :

noa bir dO əDi bOtOran-a~b t ran-ge-a 'this forest is very fearful.

uni dO dayavan-kan-a-e 'he is kind'

Era dO hErElan-a-e 'the lady is having husband'

ona OnOl dO noṅkan-ge-a 'that essay is like this'

uni dO okarEn-kan-a-e 'he is of where'

Verbal adjectives : Different types of verbal constructions are used as adjectives.

(i) Reduplicated verb stem is used as adjective; e.g.

a. As attribute :

dadal hOR 'beating man' from *dal* 'beat'

ñEñEl kuRi 'sight-having girl' from *ñEl* 'see'

gEgEr seta 'biting dog' from *gEr* 'bite'

b. As predicate complement :

nui hOR dO dadal-ge-a-e 'this man is in the habit of beating'

seta dO gEgEr-ge-a-e 'the dog is in the habit of biting'

(ii) Reciprocal verb stems are occasionally used as attributive adjectives in endocentric attributive constructions ; e.g.

gipitic' tənDi 'collective lying place' from *gitic'* 'lie'

dupuRup' tənDi 'collective sitting place' from *duRup* 'sit'

(iii) The intransitive verb roots and stems with /kan/ are used as adjectives; e.g.

calak'kan hOR 'going man' from *calak'* 'go'

hijuk'kan serma 'coming year' from *hEc'* 'come'

gujuk'kan Danra 'dying bullock' from *gOc'* 'die'

daraykan ñində 'coming night' from *daray* 'come'

(iv) Verb roots with the perfect suffix in the neutral are used as attributive adjectives; e.g.

jaRoaakan hOR 'gathered men' from *jaRoa* 'gather'

hEc'akan bOyha 'brother who has come' from *hEc'* 'come'

(v) Verb roots with the simple past tense suffix in the neutral are used as attributive adjectives ; e.g.

calaoen serma 'last year' from *calao* 'go'

parOmen mãhã 'last day' from *parOm* 'pass'

Genitive and phrasal adjectives : Nominals with genitive suffixes and /leka/ - phrases are functionally adjectives. A /leka/-phrase when used predicatively the adjectival /-n/ is suffixed to it; e.g.

a. As attribute :

oRak'-rEn bahu 'wife of the house'

dare-rEak'jO 'fruit of the tree'

am-ak' katha 'thy word'

ato-rEn manva 'man of the village'

iñ-rEn hOpOn 'my son'

baha-leka daka 'flower-like rice'

sEngEl-leka paura 'fire-like liquor'

b. As predicate complement :

nui hOpOn dO iñ-rEn-kan-a-e 'this son is mine'

jO dO noa dare-rEak'-kan-a-e 'the fruit is of this tree'

okaTak' dO am-ak'-kan-a 'which one is yours ?

daka dO baha-lekan-a 'the rice is like flower'

Types of adjectives : Somantically the adjectives may be subgrouped into two types—qualificative and quantificative.

Qualificative : The qualificative adjectives express the nature and character of the person or thing qualified. They are used both attributively and predicatively. Examples —

As attribute	As predicate complement
mañjhi/ mãjhi hOR 'head man'	*nui d mañjhi/mãjhi-kan-a-e- 'the person* is the head of the village'
bhale hOR 'good man'	*uni dO bhale-tahẼkan-a-e* 'he was good'
noṅkan kəmi 'work like this'	*uni dO noṅkan-ge-a-e* 'he is like this'

Another mark of the qualificative is its suseaptibility of modification by *adi* 'very', *tin* 'how'; e.g.

əDi bele-bili jO 'very ripe fruit'

əDi bəric' hOR 'very bad man'

tin maraṅ 'how big'

tin napay 'how nice'

Quantificative : Quantificatives express the quantity of the nouns. They are used as attributes in endocentric attributive constructions but not predicatively; e.g.

Sanam 'all' as in *sanam tənDi* 'all places'

ayma 'many' as in *ayma koRa* 'many boys'

jOtO/ jhO:O 'all' as in *jOtO/jhOtO hOR* 'all men'

tin 'how many' as in *tin bOyha* 'how many brothers'

adOm 'some' as in *adOm hOR* 'some men'

Position of adjective :

(i) Adjectives in endocentric attributive constructions precede the nominal head; e.g.

banar koRa 'both boys'

ponon hOR 'all four men'

(ii) In the subject-predicate complement sentence where the adjective is used as predicate complement it is obligatorily followed by the finite marker /a/. Sometimes the particle /ge/, /kan/ and /tahEkan/ are also used after the adjective and in these cases the finite marker comes after them; e.g.

uni dO boba-ge-a-e 'this knife is very sharp'

noa churi dO ∂Oi laser-a 'this knife is very sharp'

oñ dO rEṅgEc'-tahẼkan-a-ñ 'I was hungry'

seta dO khEpa-kan-a-e 'the god is mad'

Gender distinction : Normally the adjectives do not show gender concord with the noun qualified. But a few adjectives borrowed from the neighbouring I.A. languages (Bengali or some forms of Eastern Hindi) show two-day gender distinction — masculine and feminine. In these cases the adjectives ended in /-d/ replace /- a/ by /-i/ in the feminine and as such the adjectives ended in /- a/ are regarded as masculine. Examples —

Masculine	Feminine
kala	*k∂li* 'deaf'
koṅka	*kuṅki* 'dumb, mad'
khEpa	*khepi* 'mad'
kãRã	*kãRi* 'blind'
totra	*tutri* 'stammering'
kõda	*kũdi* 'dumb'
phogra	*phugri* 'teethless'

Morphophonological changes :

(i) When a is followed by i in the next syllable it is neutralized; e.g.

kala + i = *k∂li*

kãRã + i = *k∂Ri*

(ii) When E is followed by is in the next syllable it becomes e; e.g.

khEpa + i = *khepi*

(iii) When o is followed by i in the next syllable it becomes u; e.g.

koṅka + i = *kuṅki*

totra + i = *tutri*

kõda + i = *kũdi*

phogra + i = *phugri*

Degree of comparison :

The adjective itself is not inflected to show different degrees of comparison. Rather to obtain comparative and superlative degree the postpositions are added to the word with which something is to be compared.

To obtain comparative degree the ablative postpositions/kh n/ 'from' in the Southern dialect and /kh c'/ id' in the Northern dialect are used. /kh n/ may take the impersonal suffix /-ak'/ and then the postposition becomes /khanak'/; e.g.

Southern dialect -

nuiic' bitkli iñic'-(khOn) hõe marañ-a 'the buffalo-cow of this person is bigger even that of mine'

hana dare noa dareko-(khOn) dO sẼRa-ge-a 'that tree (yonder) is bigger than this tree'

nuiTak' marañic'-khOnak' dare-a 'this very one is stronger than the earlier one'

hana-(khOn) noa dO bhage -a 'this is better than that (yonder)'.

Northern dialect -

iñrEn kaOa-(khOc') unirEnge laTo-a-e 'his buffalo is bigger then that of mine'

noa-(khOc') hanage bhage-a 'that (yonder) is better than this'

Sometimes along with the above mentioned postpositions the morphemes *bisl* 'more', *bərti* 'id' are used before the adjectives to express the comparative degree; e.g.

S.S. *uni-(khOn) nuige bisi dare-a-e* 'this one is stronger than that one'

N.S. *noa jO ona jO-(khOc') bərti sebela-sibil-a* 'this fruit is more palatable than that'

To obtain superlative degree the same ablative postpositions/ khOn/ or /khOnak' / (Southern dialect) and /khOc' / (Northern dialect) are added to *jOtO~jhOtO* 'all' and then the comparison is made with this ; e.g.

S.S. *ul jOtO~jhOtOkhOn sebel~sibil-a* 'mango is the most palatable of all'

N.S. *uni hOR jOtO~jhOtOkhOc' usul-a* 'that man is the tallest of all'

2. Numeral

The numerals in Santali are generally found as quantifiers combined with classifiers. The actual number is denoted by the quantifiers. The quantifiers are used singly when they are used in counting or in enumerating human beings but in all other cases they are combined with classifiers which are bound morphemes and are never used alone. These two morphemes used in combination actually present the numeral system in Santali.

Some morpho-syntactic functions are performed by numerals. First, they may take certain suffixes and as such function as adverbs; e.g. *mit'* + /-tE/ -*mit'tE* 'together'; *mit'* + /-then/ = *mit'ThEn* 'in one place'. Secondly, like attributive adjectives they occur in endocentric attributive construction to qualify nouns, but like pure adjectives they do not occur as predicative adjectives; e.g.

> *bar hOR* 'two men'
> *barea Daṅra* 'two bullocks'
> *pEa koDa* 'three buffaloes'
> *mit' Tan bir* 'one forest'

Thirdly, the inclusive numerals along with their capability of being used as adjectives are also used as nouns.

Numeral classifier: The numeral classifier in Santali is a limited class of morphemes, defined by the fact that the members of the class can occur directly after the quantifier and form a word with it.

The classifiers fall into two classes, viz. human and non-human. The class human is, in turn, divided into indefinite marked by ϕ and definite. Human definite and non-human are marked by the same classifiers. The above categorization may be shown in the following diagram :

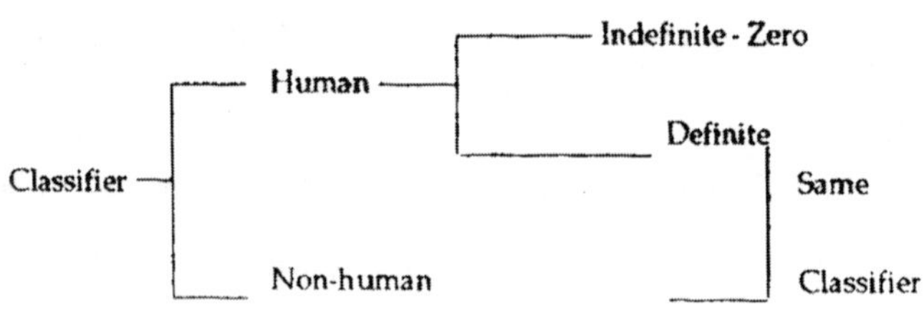

The classifiers in Santali are not used indiscriminately i.e. any classifier cannot be used with any quantifier. They have particular distribution and accordingly fall into three classes. The classifiers belonging to class I are used with the quantifier for 'one' only; the class II is used with the quantifier from 'two' through 'four' and the class III is used with the quantifiers from 'five' onwards. The last class is sometimes used with the quantifier for 'one' also, particularly in songs, perhaps 'metri causa'

The following list includes all of the common classifiers :

Class I : /Taṅ/, /TEn/, /TEc'/. These classifiers are used with the quantifier for 'one' and are used for human non-living beings, non-human living beings, non-human non-living objects, for a wide and miscellaneous variety of inanimate objects in everyday use, viz. furniture, household objects etc., for non-corporal objects like words, songs and stories, things in general and particular. The same classifiers are also used for the human/living beings when definite.

There are dialectal differences regarding the choice of the classifiers. /TEn/ and /TEc'/ are used regularly in the Northern dialect where they are in free variation. /Tan/ is the regular one in the Southern dialect.

Example —

Southern	Northern
mit'Taṅ gOc' hOR	*mit'TEc' gOc'hOR* 'one dead man'
mit'Taṅ uric'	*mit'TEc' uric'* 'one bullock'
mit'Taṅ kəli boṅga	*mit'TEn kəli boṅga* 'one kali idol'
mit'Taṅ putul	*mit'TEn putul* 'one doll'
mit'Taṅ rakkhos	*mit'TEn rakkhos* 'one man-eater'
mit'Taṅ dare	*mit'TEc' dare* 'one tree'
mit'Taṅ hatiar	*mit'TEc' hətiər* 'one weapon'
mit'Taṅ gam	*mit'TEn gam* 'one story'
mit'Taṅ ato	*mit'TEn ato* 'one village'
mit'Taṅ hOR	*mit'TEc' hOR* 'one man, (definite)

Class II : /ea/. This classifier is limited to the numerals from 'two' through 'four' and 'twenty' and are used for the non-human living beings, human non-living beings, for non-human non-living objects and also for the same objects entered in class I. The same classifier is used for the human living beings when definite. Examples —

barea boṅga	'two ghosts'
barea sim	'two cocks'
pEa putul	'three dolls'
ponea jinis	'four things'
barea katha	'two words'
pEa parkOm	'three cots'
ponea gatE	'four friends' (definite)

Class III : /goTaṅ/, /goTEc'/, /goTEn/ : Quantifiers from 'five' through 'ten' and the distributive numerals take these classifiers. There are sporadic instances of using these classifiers with the quantifier for 'one' but that is limited to songs and presumably for metrical purposes. These classifiers are used for the non-human living beings, non-human non-living objects, human non-living beings and other countable objects. The classifiers are also used for the human living beings when definite.

Dialectally, /goTaṅ/ is the common classifier in the southern dialect while /goTEn/ and /goTEc' / are in free variatiaon in the northern dialect.

The numerals can be broadly divided into primary and derived. The primary ones are (i) cardinal; (ii) ordinal; (iii) approximative and (iv) fractional. The derived ones are formed either by adding affixes and other formatives or by reduplication. They are (i) distributive, (ii) proportional and (iii) inclusive.

Cardinal numeral : There are ten basic quantifiers in Santali and those may be called the atoms of the numeral system. Further numerals from 'ten' onwards are formed from these atoms. Santali numeral system is a mixture of decimal where the quantifiers from ten onwards are formed from 'ten' either by addition or by multiplication and vigesimal where 'twenty' serves as the base for forming further quantifiers. The atoms can be enumerated as follows :

mit'	'one'	*turui*	'six'
bar	'two'	*eay*	'seven'

pE	'three'		
pon	'four'	*irəl*	'eight'
arE	'nine'		
mõRE	'five'	*gEl*	'ten'

The quantifiers from 'ten' through 'nineteen' are formed by adding the quantifiers for 'one' to 'nine' to the base 'ten' and hence the quantifier for 'ten' is the augend i.e., that which is added to and the quantifiers from 'one' to 'nine' which are added to form the intermediate quantifiers i.e. from 'eleven' to 'nineteen' are addends. The addends usually occur after the base. Thus we find

gEl mit'	'eleven'	*gEl turu*	'sixteen'
gEl bar	'twelve'	*gEl eay*	'seventeen'
gEl pE	'thirteen'	*gEl irəl*	'eighteen'
gEl pon	'fourteen'	*gEl arE*	'nineteen'
gEl mõRE	'fifteen'		

The decades from 'twenty' onwards are the result of multiplication. Here we find two types of formations – in one case, the quantifier for 'ten' serves as the multiplicand i.e. that which is multiplied and the basic numeral function as multiplier i.e. that which multiplies, thus —

bar gEl = $2 \times 10 = 20$ *turui gEl* = $6 \times 10 = 60$
pE gEl = $3 \times 10 = 30$ *eay gEl* = $7 \times 10 = 70$
pon gEl = $4 \times 10 = 40$ *iral gEl* = $8 \times 10 = 80$
mõrE gEl = $5 \times 10 = 50$ *arE gEl* = $9 \times 10 = 90$

Regarding the position of the multiplier and the multiplicand, the multiplier usually precedes the multiplicand. Here, in the above examples where 'ten' is the serialized multiplicand there is a separate quantifier for hundred viz. *say sO* 'hundred' *say* being used absolutely and *sO* contextually, which is normally the case in the decimal system.

In the other type there is a separate quantifier for 'twenty viz. *isi* which serves as the serialized multiplicand for further decades. In this case the round decades (i.e. 40, 60, 80, 100) are formed by the simple multiplication of the base, and the odd decades (i.e. 30, 50, 70, 90) are the results of the combination of multiplication with addition.

Thus —

mit'isi $= 1 \times 20 = 20$ *pE isi* $= 3 \times 20 = 60$

bar isi $= 2 \times 20 = 40$ *pon isi* $= 4 \times 20 = 80$

morE isi $= 5 \times 20 = 100$

mit' isi gl $= 1 \times 20 + 10 = 30$

bar isi gl $= 2 \times 20 + 10 = 50$

pE isi gl $= 3 \times 20 + 10 = 70$

pon isi gl $= 4 \times 20 + 10 = 90$

The intermediate quantifiers between decades from 'twenty' onwards are also the result of combination of multiplication with addition. Here also the same two systems survive, i.e. both decimal and vigesimal occur as the base and to the base the quantifiers from 'one' through 'nine' are added to derive the intermediate ones. In these composite quantifiers the multiplier precedes and the addend follows the multiplicand; thus —

Type II *mit'isi mit'* $= 1 \times 20 + 1 = 21$

Type I *bar gEl mit'* $= 2 \times 10 + 1 = 21$

Type II *mit'isi bar* $= 1 \times 20 + 2 = 22$

Type I *bar gEl bar* $= 2 \times 10 + 2 = 22$

Type II *mit'isi gEl mit'* $= 1 \times 20 + 10 + 1 = 31$

Type I *pE gEl mit'* $= 3 \times 10 + 1 = 31$

Type II *bar isi turui* $= 2 \times 20 + 6 = 46$

Type I *pon gEl turui* $= 4 \times 10 + 6 = 46$

The quantifier *mit'* 'one' generally precedes 'twenty' and 'hundred' to indicate that 'twenty' or 'hundred' is taken as the unit.

Cardinal numeral and language contact : Santali being a neighbour of the eastern Indo-Aryan languages, viz. Bengali, Assamese, Oriya and Eastern Hindi, has direct contact with these languages and their speakers. Staying side by side with the speakers of these alien languages and having direct contact it has borrowed, among other linguistic features, the numerals. Both in the northern and the southern dialects commonly the Santali numerals upto 'six' are preserved and further numerals, say from 'seven' onwards are borrowed from these IA languages. Mostly the speakers of the southern dialect cannot recognize the original Santali numerals above 'six' and counting goes on in IA numerals.

But in the northern dialect the speakers can recognise the original numerals beyond 'six' and occasionally use them, though for practical purposes the IA numerals are used and in this system *isi* is 'twenty'. The numerals from 21 through 26 are formed by adding the original numerals to the base *mit' isi* 20 and from 27 through 39 the numerals are formed by adding IA numerals to the base *mit'isi* 'twenty'. In this way the first six original numerals are added to the round base i.e. 40, 60, 80, 100 and the further ones added are Indo-Aryan.

Ordinal numeral and language contact : Santali has no original ordinal numeral and it is quite interesting that there is no ordinal like 'first', 'second', 'third' etc. where there are numerals for 'one' 'two' and so on.

Santali has three borrowed ordinal numerals from IA and they are *pəhil-polio* 'first', *dOsar* 'second' and *tesar* 'third'. They are used as attributes in an endocentric attributive construction and also as adverbs; e.g. as attribute : *pəhil koRa* 'first boy'

[as adverb *pəhil jOmlem* 'eat first']

In the northern dialect, when it becomes necessary the common cardinals with the suffix /-ic'/ for the animate and /-ak'/ for the inanimate are used as such and in this way the first three borrowed ordinals mention above are also affected. Thus—

Animate	**Inanimate**
pəhilic' 'first'	*pəhilak'* 'first'
dOsaric' 'second'	*dOsarak'* 'second'
tesaric' 'third'	*tesarak'* 'third'
ponic' 'fourth'	*ponak'* 'fourth'
mõREic' 'fifth'	*mõREak'* 'fifth'
turuiic' 'sixth'	*turuiak'* 'sixth'
eayic' 'seventh'	*eayak'* 'seventh'
irəlic' 'eighth'	*irəlak'* 'eighth'
arEic' 'ninth'	*arEak'* 'ninth'
gElic' 'tenth'	*gElak'* 'tenth'

Approximative numeral : The approximative numerals are expressed by using side by side the two consecutive numerals approximated, the higher numeral being preceded by the lower with or without any conjunctive link in between; thus —

bar pE 'two or three'

pE pon 'three or four'

Some speakers trying to be more deliberate and analytic use in overt conjunctive between the two numerals, thus—

bar sE pE 'two or three'

pon sE mõRE 'four or five'

mõR E sE turui 'five or six'

Some times also a term for approximation is used with the numeral; thus *-pasEc' mit'* say 'about one hundred'

Fractional numeral : Santali has only one fractional numeral expression and that is *tara* or *adha* for half, *adha* being borrowed from IA.

Sometimes the expressions like

bar hɘTiñ-rEak' mit'hɘTiñ'	one of two divisions'
pon haTiñ-rEak' mit'hɘTiñ	'one of four divisions'
pE hɘTiñ-rEak' bar hɘTiñ	'two of three divisions'

as fractional numerals are used but they are rather very uncommon.

Distributive numeral : Distributive numerals from 'one' through 'five' are formed by reduplicating the initial consonant along with the vowel; thus —

mit' 'one'	*mimit'* 'one each'
bar 'two'	*babar* 'two each'
pE 'three'	*pEpE* 'three each'
pon 'four'	*popon* 'four each'
*mõ*RE 'five'	*mOmOR* 'five each'

Bodding[2] has shown the formation of the distributive numerals from 'one' through 'ten' in this way. But in my data the formation of the distrubutive numerals in this way is restricted to the first five numerals only. The other distributives are formed by adding / katE / after the cardinal numerals along with the classifiers. This type of formation is also not rare in case of the first five distributives; thus —

mit'Tan katE	'one each' (Southern dialect.)
mit'TEn-TEc' katE	'id' (northern dialect.)
pEa katE	'three each'
ponea katE	'four each'
mõREgoTan katE'	'five each (Southern dialect)
mõREgOTEn~gOTEc' katE	'id' (Northern dialect)
turuigoTan katE	'six each' (Southern dialect)
turuigOtEn~gOTEc' katE	'id' (Northern dialect)
gElgoTan katE	'ten each' (Southern dialect)
gElgOTEn-gOTEc' katE	'id' (Northern dialect).

The reduplicated distributive numerals very often require the classifiers /goTan/, /gOTEn/ and /gÓTEc'/. Sometimes the classifiers for the respective cardinal numerals are used instead of /goTan/, /gOTEc'/ and /gOTEn/. Sometimes /katE/ is also added after the numeral classifiers or directly after the reduplicated distributive numerals; thus —

Southern dialect	**Northern dialect**
mimit' gotan 'one each'	*mimit' gOTEc'gOTEn* 'one each'
babar goTan 'two each'	*babar gOTEn* 'two each'
babar goTan kate 'id'	*babar gOTEn katE* 'id'
babar katE 'id'	*babar katE* 'id'
mimit' Tan mimit'Tan katE 'one each'	*mimit TEn mimit Ten kate* 'one each'
babarea babarea katE 'two each'	*babarea babarea katE* 'two each'

Repetitive numeral : Repetitive numerals are formed by adding /dhao/ or /dOm/ to the basic numerals; e.g.

mit'dhao~dOm	'once'
bar dhao~ dOm	'twice'
pE dhao~dOm	'thrice'
eaydhao~dOm	'seven times'
gEl dhao~dOm	'ten times'

They are used as adverbs.

Inclusive numeral : Santali possesses three inclusive numerals, viz. *banar* 'both', *pEnE* 'all three' and *ponon* 'all four'. They have dual functions, first, like nouns they are used as subject or object of a sentence.

banar-ge dal-kin-nE 'beat both'

pEnE agu-akat' -ko-a-ñ 'I have brought all three'

and second, they are used as attributes in endocentric attributive constructions; e.g.

ponon kombRo 'all four thieves'

Morphophonological Changes

(i) t' of *mit'* becomes / n / before another morpheme beginning with h; e.g.

mit' hOR = / min hOR /

mit' hOpta = / min hOpta /

(ii) a. r of *banar* is lost before another morpheme beginning with h; e.g. *banar hOR* = / bana hOR /

b. e of the classifier / ea / is dropped after a numeral ending in vowel; e.g.

pE + / ea / = / pEa /.

References

1. Some of the adjectives have counterparts with high vowels along with the mid-high as *thobro~thubru* 'blunt', sebel_sibil 'palatable'. Both the pronunciations are given.
2. P.O. Bodding, Materials for a Santali Grammar II. Dnmka : Santal Mission of the Northern Churches, 1929, p.60.

6

ADVERB

Adverb, in Santali, irrespective of their position in a sentence are modifiers. In some cases they modify the verb and sometimes the whole clause.

Formation of Adverbs : On the formal domain the adverbs may be classified into three classes, viz. (i) simple; (ii) derivative and (iii) miscellaneous.

Simple Adverbs : To this category belong a number of words, simple and indecomposable, functioning as adverbs; e.g.

usəra 'quickly' *usəra kəmi-mE* 'do quickly'

dOme 'very much' *dOme-ko rak'-ed-a* 'they are crying very much'

lOgOn 'hurriedly' *lOgOn hatao-mE* 'take hurriedly'

eskar 'alone' eskar tahEn bañ boge-a 'staying alone is not good'

nahak' 'presently' *nahak'-e hijuk'-a* 'he will go presently'

tis 'when' *tis-em hijuk'-a* 'when will you come?

nit[1] 'now' *nit-ge uni-rEn Dañra-ko ətkir-et' -ko-a* 'right now they are running away with his bullocks'

čOT 'immediately' *hOhOcOT-e hEc'-gOt'-en-a* 'Immediately on being called he came' *laha* 'first, previously' *laha Dańra ∂gu-le-kin-mE* 'first being the two bullocks'

un 'then' *uni un-e hEc'-len-a* 'then he came'.

cedak' 'why' *cedak'-em r∂sk∂k'- kan-a* 'why are you rejoicing ?'

nEtar 'at present' *nEtar onko/unku hoRo-ko cas-ed-a* 'at present they are cultivating paddy'

nes 'this year' *nEs uni oRak'-e hijuk'-a* 'this year he will come home'

seday 'in old days' *seday onko/unku buluń-ko benao-et' 'tahẼc/ tahẼkana* 'in old days they were making salt'

acka 'suddenly' *acka-e ñur-en-a* 'he fell down suddenly'

p∂hil (N.S.) 'at first' *pEra p∂hil Em-le-ko-pE* 'at first give to the guests'

poilo (S.S.) 'id' *pEra poilo Em-le-ko-pE* 'id'

din∂m 'daily' *din∂m-ge-e dal-iń- a* 'he beats me daily'

enań 'then' *enań in dal-e-kan-tahẼc'/tahẼkana* 'then I was beating him'.

marań 'at first' *marań l∂i-le-m* 'tell first'

bhage 'well' *unku/onko dO bhage-ko bic∂r-ed- a* 'they are judging well'

dhin∂ń 'after a while' *dhin∂ń hijuk'-mE* 'come a little after'

jãhã 'any where' *jãhã-ge sEnOk'-a* 'go anywhere'

Derivative adverbs : Adverbs which are formed from demonstrative elements, interrogative pronouns and numerals adding formative elements are grouped under derivative adverbs. Demonstrative adverbs of manner, interrogative adverbs of manner (only one instance) — a hapaxlegomenon and adverb of frequency fall in to this category.E.G.

nońka 'thus' *nońka alo-m rOR-a* 'do not say thus'

onkatE 'in that way manner' *onka-tE∂di din pOlOm-en-a* 'many days are gone in that way'

onka 'in that way' *onka k∂mi-mE* 'do in that way'

hankatE 'in that way' *hanka-tE curok'-mE* 'go round that way'

hanka 'id' *hanka-ko galmarao-kan-a* 'they are conversing that way' *neṅka/niṅkə* 'just in this way' *neṅka ləi-mE* 'say (just) in this way'

onka/inkə 'just in that way' *enka/inkə-barE tahE-oco/hOcO-a-m* 'let it remain thus'

ceka/cikə 'how' *ceka/cikə hoyuk'- a* 'how it will be/how it is?

ceka/cikə-tE-m calak-a 'how will you go?'

mit'dhao 'once' *uni mit'dhao hEc'-lena* 'he came once'

To this miscellaneous class belong different types of formations which are used as adverbs.

a. Words with the suffix /-tE/ are used as adverbs :

usəratE hEc'-en-a-e	'he came quickly'
lOgOntE hijuk'-mE	'come hurriedly'
maraṅtE jOm-le-m	'cat first'
cãrtE kami-mE	'do sincerely'
uni cãrtE ñEl-an-a-e	'he watched sincerely'
ekkaltE-a rOR-gOt'-ked-a	'he spoke instantly'
uni bOtOrtE dəR-led-a-e	'he had fled in fear'
kusitE-ñ rəskək'-kan-a	'I am rejoicing in joy'
kuRi dO bhabnatE rarak'-kan-a-e	'the young lady is crying in grief'
mit' tE-ko sendra calao-len-a	'they had gone together for hunting'
sOṅgEtE ona joron jaṅ-rE harta hoi-gOt'-en-a	'at once skin grew in that joined bone'
LshayE-laṅ jOm-le-ge tayOmtE-laṅ calak'-a	'first we (dl) eat afterwards we will go'.

b. Words with the suffix /-rE/ are used as adverbs :

tinrE gOc'-en-a-e 'when he died ?

unrEn dal-e-kan-tahẼc'/tahẼkan-a 'then I was beating him'

laharE uni gidrə dal-e-a-e 'first beat that boy'

uni laharE mena-e-a 'he is in front'

samanrE henak'-a 'it is there in front'

tayOmrE OkOe hO bənuk'-ko-a	'there are none in the back'
dak' sur-sorrE menak'-a	'water is near'
bhitrirE dOhO -akan-a	'it kept in side'

c. **Reduplicated words with the suffix/-tE/ are used as adverbs :**

pəri pəritE kəmi-mE	'do by turns'
bəi bəitE harak'-a	'it will grow gradually'
mOnE mOnEtE mEn-an-a-e	'he said in mind'

d. **Reduplicated words are used as adverbs :**

/ kəc'kəc' dak'-et'-tahẼkanea-e	'it was raining a little'
lOgOn lOgOn sEnOk'-mE	'go quickly'
uni ghəRic' ghəRic'-e hijuk'-kan-a ar calak'-kan-a	'he is constantly coming and going'
jhOmOr jhOmOr-e dadak'-kan-a	'it is raining heavily'
jadOm jadam dak'-ed-a	'it is raining continuously'

e. **Words along with their echo counterparts are used as adverbs:**

hakopako hijuktaE	'come quickly'
əTupəTu kami-mE	'do quickly'
harEpharE saprak'-mE	
cãrE mãrE dhuti hOdOk'-mE	
/jãhãtãhã alom gitij-a/	

f. **Geminated verb stems with the suffix /-tE/ are used as adverbs.**

sEnOk' sEnOk'tE-e mEn-ked-a'while going he said'

sereñ sereñtE-e calak'kan-tahẼc' / tahẼkana'while going he was singing'

calaO calaotE birdhare-rE jaṅ-ko ñam-ked-a'while going they got the bone beside the forest'

uni rak'rak'tE calak'kan-a-e'while crying he is going'

iñ am-sOṅgE katha mEn mEntE hEc'-len-a'while talking with you I had come'

In the southern dialect /-tE/ is added to the geminated intransative verb roots, as *sEn sEntE* 'while going', *calao calaotE* 'while going', while in the northern dialect /-tE/ is added to the geminated intransitive verb stems, as *calak' calak'tE* 'while going' *sEnOk' sEnOk'tE* 'while going'. There is no such variation in case of the transitive verbs.

Type of adverb : Semantically, adverbs may be classified into the following groups : (i) adverb of manner; (ii) adverb of location and direction; (iii) adverb of time; (iv) causal adverbs and (v) adverb of frequency.

(i) Adverbs of manner are used to modify the verb and the sentence

usəra	'quickly'	*lOgOn*	'huriedly'
usəratE		*lOgOntE*	
		lOgOn lOgOn	
eskar 'alone'		*bəi bəitE*	'slowly'
pəripəritE 'by turns'		*hakopako*	
harEpharE 'quickly'		*ətupətu*	
cārEmārE 'sincerely'		*ghəRic' ghəRic'*	'incessantly'
cārE 'sincerely'		*mit'tE*	'together'
ekkaltE 'at once, instantly'	*nonka*		'thus'
onka 'in that way'		*hanka*	'in that way'
nenka ninka '(just) 'thus'		*enka inka*	'in that way'
ceka - cikə 'how'			

(ii) Adverbs of location and direction generally modify the whole sentence

	sorrE surrE	'near'
	laharE	'in front'
cOTtE 'upwards'	*tayOmrE*	'behind'
bhitrirE 'inside'	*samanrE*	'in front'

(iii) Adverb of time

nahak'	'presently'	*tis*	'on what day, when'
nit	'now'		
tinrE	'when, at what time'	*enan*	'a little while age'
dinəm	'daily'	*nEtar*	'now-a-days'
dhinən	'a little after'	*seday*	'in old days'

nEs	'this year'	*un*	'then'
pəhil-poilo	'formerly'	*unrE*	
maraṅ *maraṅtE*	'previously, before'		
laha *lahatE*	'formerly, before'		

tayOmtE 'afterwards'

(iv) Causal adverb

bOtOrtE 'in fear'

bhabnatE 'in grief'

kusitE 'in joy'

rəskətE 'in joy'

(v) Adverb of frequency

mit'dhao~dOm	'once'
bardhao~dOm	'twice'
pondhao~dOm	'four times'
tindhao~dOm	'how many times'

The postposition / leka / 'like' may be used with the demonstrative adverbs of manner, *noṅka, onka, hanka, neṅka/niṅkə* and *enka/inka* resulting in *noṅka leka, onka leka, hanka leka, neṅka leka,/niṅkə enka leka/inkə leka* without any difference in meaning and use. The addition of the suffix /-tE/ to these i.e. *noṅka leka, onka leka* etc. gives emphasis to the manner in which the action takes place. e.g.

noṅka lekatE tahẼoco/hOcO-ae- mE	'let him stay in this very manner'
onka lekatE mEn-mE sE	'say in that very manner'
hanka lekatE calaocco/hOcO-ae-mE	'let him go in that very manner'
neṅka/niṅkə lekatE calak' baṅ ganok	*'-a* 'it will not be possible to go in this very manner.
enka-inkə lekatE bujhau-ked-e-a-ñ	'I made him understand in that very manner'

The postposition /leka/ 'like' can also be added to the inanimate interrogative pronoun *cet'/cit* 'what', along with the suffix /-tE/ carrying the meaning 'in what manner, e.g.

cet'/cit' 'lekatE calao hoyuk'-a	'how, in what manner going will be done'

The suffix /-tE/ is also added to *nońka, onka, hanka, neńka ninkə, enka inka, ceka cikə* giving the sense of direction in which the action will take place; e.g.

nońkatE sEnOk'-mE	'go by thus'
onkatE hijuk'-mE	'come by that way'
hankatE rORgOt'-ked-a-e	'he spoke in that manner, way'.
ceka-cikətE-m rOR-a	'how will you speak'
enka-inkətE dak' calao-en-a-e	'it rained in that direction'

The postposition /katE/ can also be added to the manner adverbs giving the sense of (doing' resembling the adverbial formation of Bengali in /koria/ or /kore/ :

nońka katE idiy-mE	'take away in this way manner'
onka katE duRup'-mE	'sit in that manner'
cekakatE -cikəkatE hoyuk'-a	'how it will be done'.

7

PARTICLE

Santali has a good number of particles though not so large as compared with other grammatical classes. The forms belonging to this class are neither free nor bound. They are not free as their occurrences are sentence-bound and not bound like affixes and postpositions for they are almost always preceded and followed by open juncture. Besides the native ones Santali has borrowed some words from the neighbouring Indo-Aryan languages which are deemed as particles.

Some of the particles, e.g. negative, affirmative, invitative, temporal, adversative, interrogative, conjunctive and disjunctive have their independent meaning. But some particles are untranslatable and their meaning depends on their syntax. Certain particles like ordinary negative, affirmative and interrogative when occur alone express a complete idea, hence correspond to a sentence, thus —

baṅ	'no'
hẽ	'yes'
ki	'what'?
cedak'	'why'

Santali particles can be divided into the following groups depending on the different functions they perform in a sentence :

Negative : There are three negative particles - /baṅ/ as ordinary negative, /alo/ as prohibitive negative and /oho/ as emphatic negative. All of them occur in the preverb position and in all the three cases the suffixed forms of the personal pronouns are added to them instead of the verb to mark the animate subject. The ordinary negative /baṅ/ drops its final consonant when the suffixed forms of the subject pronouns are added to it though exceptions are not rare.

/baṅ/ : It is used in ordinary negative sentences and also in conditional clauses in which the protasis will or may take place, takes place or has taken place.

unku ba-ko~ban-ko baDay-a 'they do not know'

alE ba-lE~aṅ-lE sEnOK'-a 'we (pl.) will not go'

iñ ba-ñ baDay-a 'I do not know'

unkin hõ adõ ba-kin baṅ-kin dəR-led-a 'even they (dl) had not run then'

jodi uni lahatE ba-e 'If he would not come out earlier'

pnDp-kok'-a tahle hande ba-e tiyok'-ke-a 'he might not reach there (yonder)'

EnrE hõuni gidrə do ba-m goc' dare-ad-e- a 'even then you could

apE birutE ba-pE calak'kana 'are you (pl) not going to Biru ?'

setoṅ situṅrE hor baṅ ñElOk'-kan-a 'the road is not seen in the dark'

noa do baṅ jOmOK'-a 'this will not be eaten'

/baṅ/ when occurs alone is used as a negative answer, thus— *ceka, aben birutE ba-baṅ calak'-a ?* 'What, will you (dl) not go to Biru ?' *ban* 'no'

/alo/ : It indicates prohibition and occurs in the simple present / future verb forms with second person and verb forms with *alo* performs the function of the negative imperative. Example—

handE alo-m calaK'-a 'do not go there'

alo-ben/bin rOR-a 'do not speak'

setońi-situńrE alo-m dəR-baray-a	'do not run in the sun'
siñbEra alo-m japid-a	'do not sleep by day'
iskul alo-pE calak'-a	'do not go to school'

There is only one instance in my data – *khub sOktOkatE tOlmE, jEmOn alo laRa* 'tie it very hard, so that it may not be loosened' where it is used in a final clause and loses its prohibitive sense, Again, the general preverb position of the negative finds its alternative in this particular instance.

/oho/ : It is an emphatic negative used with the subjunctive verb forms and with another aspect in the apodosis part of a conditional sentence. Examples —

iñ a dO OhOñ lәi-ke-a 'I might not say'

unku-ko lәi-ed-a 'alE lәi benao-dare-ae-a tobe jivi dO OhO-lE Em-ke-a' 'they are saying, 'we can make him by uttering mystical formula but we are unable to give him life'

iñ do nui gidrә OhO-ñ gOc'dare-ke-a	'I am unable to kill this boy'
bin damtE noaOhOñ Em-le-ke-a	'I shall certainly not give them this without being paid for it'
ba-m dal-li-ñ-khan OhO -ñ dal-le-m-a	'if you did not beat me I would certainly not beat you'
ba-m hEc' len-khae' OhO-ñ sEn-len-a	'if he had not come I would certainly not have gone'
uni ba-e Em-li-ñ-khan OhO-n Em-le-a	'if he doesn't give me I won't give him'

Affirmative : There are three affirmative particles, all being used in the same context. All occur in the sentence-initial position as the answer of yes-no type questions.

/hẼ / hoi~h y /̰ : / hoi/ and /hOy/ are found in Southern Santali along with *hẼ* while *hẼ* is predominent in the northern dialect. The particles when used alone express each a complete idea.

Q. *iskul-tE -m calak'-a*? 'Will you go to school ?'

N.S.

A. *hẼ, iskul-tEñ calak'-a* 'Yes, I go, shall go to school'

N.S. Q. *ñEl-em hec'-akan-a* 'Have you come to see'

A. *hẼ iñ nEl-iñ hec'-akan-a* 'Yes, I have come to see'

Q. *cele, am dO hOR-tE-m rOR-a ?* 'Is it so, (that) you speak Santali ?

A. *hẼ iñ do hOR-tE-ñ rOR-a* 'Yes, I speak Santali'

Q. *ona-ge-ñ kuli'-ket'-iñ-a?* 'Did you ask me about that?'

S.S.

A. *hoi, ona-ge ñ kuli'-ket'-iñ-a?* 'Yes, I asked you about that'

Invitative

/dEla/: It occurs in the sentence-initial position with the anterior aspect with the emphatic particle /ge/ and without the finite/a/. in first person dual and plural inclusive, the subject pronoun being added to it.

dEle-bon khel-len-ge 'come, let us play'

dEla-bon jOm-le-ge 'come, let us eat'

dEla-bon jəpit'-le-ge 'come, let us (dl) sleep'

It is also used in the sentence-initial position with the ordinary verb form without the finite/a/ to denote invitation.

dEla-bon haku hako sap' 'come, let us catch fish'

It also occurs in the preverb position with the imperative verb form. The subject pronoun is not added to it.

baha mai dEla hijuk'-mE 'O phulmani, come'

When used alone it indicates an invitation to come.

dEla : 'come' :

/diloi/ : It is used in that particular context when the response to the invitation is not immediate. It is used with the imperative verb form in the preverb position.

diloi hijuk'-mE 'come (not immediately)'

/do~du/ : It occurs in the sentence-initial and preverb position with the imperative verb form and denote persuasion or invitation.

do~du əgu calak'-mE 'come, go to fetch'

do~du bOlO calak'-mE 'go, enter'

hili dəi do~du' ruəRjOn-mE	O sister-in-law; come make me return'

/ma/ : It occurs in the preverb position with the imperative verb form, within the verb in the optative verb forms. It generally softens the imperative into an optative sense.

ma mEn-mE	'come, speak'
ma sEnOk'-mE	'come, go'
dakakok'-ma-e	'may he prepare rice'
rOR-ma-e	'may he speak'

/cOlO/ (cp. Bengali cOlO) : It occurs in the sentence initial and preverb position with the simple present / future verb forms in the first person dual and plural inclusive.

cOlO disOm daran-bon calak'-a	'come, we will go for a visit to the country'
cOlO-lañ jOm-a	'come, we will eat'

It also occurs with the anterior aspect in first person dual and plural inclusive.

cOlO-bon sEn-len-ge	'come, let us go'
cOlO-lañ rəput'-le-ge	'come, let us break it'

Emphatic : There are three emphatic particles, /ge/, /ma/, /dO/ and /to/.

/ge/ : It is bound morpheme being always closely attached to the words emphasized. It occurs with the subject NP, object NP? with the verb and adverb. In the verb it is incorporated between the tense/aspect markers and the finite /a/. in all other cases it is postposed.

am-ge-m calak'-a	'you (not any other person) go/will go'
unku pE hOR on a katha-ge-ko hE manao-ked-a	'all three of them said yes to that (particular) word'
hEc'-en-ge-a-e'	he has come (not done any other thing)'
onka-ge calak'-m	'go thus (not in any other way)'
alE nOndE-ge-lE tahEn-a	'we stay/will stay here (not in any other place)'

/dO/. Like /ge/ it is not bound as it is preceded and followed by open juncture with stresses on it. It emphasizes that part of the sentence after which it occurs.

uni do dəR-akad-a-e 'he has run away'

nitok'do pEisi serma hoyuk'-kan-a 'it is now being sixty years'

uni gidrə do bam 'do coming'

hijuk'-kana

/to/. CP. Beng, Hindi *to_*. It occurs with the subject NP to emphasize giving it an expletive sense.

am to hola-m hEc'-akan-a 'you, it is known have come yesterday'

(cp. Bengali-*tumi to kal esecho'*

(*Hindi - hamlog to kar kharid hai* 'we are buying car')

iñ to jojom-iñ duRup'-akan-a, okoe mErom-e əgu-e-a

'I have apparently, sat to eat, who will bring the goat'

Temporal :

/ado/ 'then, thereupon'. It occurs in the sentence--initial, modial and preverb position. It never starts "discourse. In the discourse it goes with what is new rather than with what is given.

adOtopon somOy uni buohi dO ona aloye sap'-ked-a 'thereupon at the time of bath that old lady caught hold of that light'

montri hOpOn adO kisər hOpOn-e beret'-ked-e- a 'the son of the minister then roused the son of the rich man'

ar uni rakkhOs adO-e dəR-ked -a 'and that man- eater then ran away' /khan/:

The bare /khan/ is used as such in the northern dialect denoting 'then, thereupon', where it is used in the sentence-initial position introducing the continuation of a previous statement in the discourse.

khan koRa-gidrə rOrruəR-ked-a, hEnda baba ona gundli ma bili jut-akan-a 'then the boy replied, 'O father, that gundli has been ripe'.

khan dOsar hilok'-ge setak'-rE gidra-e matae-kan-a 'dE- lañ-ta sik'-lañ idi-a 'then the very second day he is telling the son in the morning 'come, son, we will go for ploughing' *khan ayo-e mEn-ked-a 'sanam khEt-ban si caba-ked-a* 'then the lady told'you have ploughed up all the field'

/khan/ in conjunction with the demonstrative root *en* 'that' in the Southern dialect and *in* 'that' in the Northern dialect meaning 'after that' is also used as a temporal particle

N.S. *enkhaniñ calak'a* 'then I shall go'

S.S. *inkhan-iñ calak'a* 'id'.

/jOkhOn/ : (op. Bengali jOkhOn) 'when'. It occurs in both the dialects.

jOkhOn uniñ metaekan tahẼkana unjokhan uni bhagi kəc'tE aj met' tahẼkanae 'when I was telling him then he was hearing attentively'

amak' isi do jOkhOn siok'ben jORaoidia unjakhEn gidrə dO lahakaem 'when you will join your plough then keep the boy infront'

/tarpOre/ : (cp. Bengali tarpOre) 'then'. It is used only in the Southern dialect and occurs in the sentence-initial position. It never occurs in starting discourse but rather sums up the previous statement in the discourse.

pEpon mãhã uniak' bÕhOk' hasoekan tahẼc' tarpOre uni dO gOc'enae 'he was suffering from headache for three or four days, then he died'.

lahatE jOmlem tarpOrelañ calak'a 'first take your food then we will go'

Conditional:

/khac'/ /khan/ :

(i) It is a bound morpheme used with the verb forms in the simple past in neutral, with the anterior aspect in active and neutral and simple present / future verb forms introducing the protasis. In all cases the finite / a/ is not added. /khac'/ is predominant in the Northern dialect with sporadic uses of /khan/. /khan/ is the only form found in the Southern dialect.

N.S. *am em hukumen-khac' noa ban kəmikea* 'if you order I would not do it'

N.S. *jodi Thik damiñ ñamle-khac' pasac' in əkhriñkikingea* If I get actual price I would probably sell the two (animate)

S.S. *bañ calaolen-khan uni bae hEc'kok'a* 'if I had not gone he would not have come'

S.S. *am bam hoho inkhan nurkok'an* 'unless you call me I would have fallen'

S.S. *bañ calaolen-khan unisalak' ñEpEl bañ hoikok'a* 'if I had not gone, meeting with him would not have happened'

S.S. *ñElle-khan-geñ dalea* 'if I find I shall beat him'

N.S. + S. S. *bam kəmi-khan tahlen chaDaomsa* 'if you do not work I shall discharge you'

/jodi/ (cp. Bengali *jodi*) 'if' : It occurs in sentence- initial modial and preverb positions introducing the protasis of a conditional sentence.

jodi uni lahatE bae onDokok'a tahle handE uni bae tiyok'kea 'if he would not come out earlier he would not reach there'

iñ jodi unkuic' gidrə ban bancaokea tahle gOc'kok'ae 'if I would not save their child then it would have died'

jodi Thik damiñ ñamkea tahleñ əkhriñkikina 'if I would get actual price then I would have sold the two (animate)'

jodi bañ calaolenkhan unisalak' ñEpEl bañ hoikok'a 'if I would not go, meeting with him would not have happened'

jodi-m calaolenkhan iñ bañ calaokok'a 'if you would go I would not have gone'

Illative:

/tObe/ (cp. Bengali tObe) 'then' : It introduces the apodosis of a conditional sentence.

jodipE uddhariña tobe apEic' gatEpEñamea 'if you (pl) rescue me then you will get your friend'

/tObe/ in conjunction with /khan/ serves the same purpose.

iñ jodi gidrə bañ bancaokea tObekhan gOc'kok'ae 'if I would not save the child then it would have died'

iñ jodi bañ calaokok'a tObekhan bae hEc' kok'a 'if I would not go then he would not have come'

/tahle/ (cp. Bengali tahole) 'then': It is sometimes used to introduce the apodosis of a conditional sentence. It is also used in conjunction with /khan/.

jodi Thik damiñ ñamkea tahleñ əkhriñkikina 'if I would get actual price then I could have sold the two'

am jodi bam kamia tahlekhan don bəgikema 'if you do not work then I shall dismiss you'

Adversative:

/menkhan/ : 'but' composed of *men* 'say' and /khan/ 'if', hence 'if it (is) said, but' etc. It occurs at the clause-initial position and serves as co-ordinating conjunct.

iñ dO uniñ ñElledea menkhan- e at'lena 'I had seen him but (then) he was lost

menkhan cikə katE/cekakatE-e mit'din uni hORrEn oRak'boṅga dO bOhOk' lac' haso ñamkedea 'but one day the wife of that man anyhow got headache and stomach pain'

ñElledeañ, menkhan bañ galmaraoadea 'I had seen him but did not speak to him'

/baṅkhan/ : It is composed of the negative particle /baṅ/ 'not' and the conditional particle /khan/ 'if', hence, 'if not, otherwise'.

onka dO alom rORa, baṅkhanlaṅ dalmea 'do not speak thus, otherwise we (dl) will beat you'

iñ daṅri əkhriñkhaniñ əkhriñkiña baṅkhan do baṅ 'If I can sell the cow I shall see, otherwise not'

nui gidra dO jãhãsEn idioTokaem, baṅkhan gOc'kaemE 'take away this boy anywhere otherwise kill him to get out of the way'

calak' añ baṅkhan cet'iñ cekay/cikəya 'I will go, if not what will I do ?'

/bickom/ : rather'

nitok' dO bickom bañ calak'a 'rather I shall not go now'

marsalkhOn bickom ñutko duləRkeda 'they loved darkness rather than light'

bOrOṅ/ : (cp. Bengali *boroṅ*) 'rather'

hoR do Dher dO bako sEnlena, 'Santals had not gone there'

bOrOṅ deko diku bərtigeko tahẼkana huge in number rather there were many Hindus'

/hutkə/ : It is used in conditional sentences to introduce the apodosis in which the protasis is supposed not to have been realised, and, therefore, the apodosis would not have occured.

nOnDEm tahẼlenkhan hutkə baren OhOe gOc'lena 'if thou hadst been here he would not have died'

amem kuliñkhan hutkə-ñ Emkema 'if thou hadst asked me I would have given it to you'

Copulative: /ar/ (cp. Bengali *ar*) 'and' : It is used to connect words phrases and sentences. It is also used in the sentence-initial position for continuing a discourse.

raja ar hOR 'the king and the man'

birsə ar iñliñ calak'a 'Birsa and I will go'

uniic' oRak'gomke ar ədiustər gidrəko tahẼkana 'there were his wife and many children'

iñ jodi mantariñ ləia ar dak'iñ chitkəua noa jaṅko joRongodok'a 'if I utter mystical formula and sprinkle water these bones will be joined'

ona ãjomsaot uni ayo dO ədie raṅgaogOt'ena ar bodget'kin jhograena 'hearing that his wife became angry and they (dl) quarreled much'

ar nit hÕ setak'ena 'and the dawn approached by this time (continued discourse).

Distunctive: /sE/ : 'or'

iñ sE am 'I or you'

ãjOmkedam sE-m baṅa 'did you hear or not'

Indefinite : /coṅ/ : It is a postpositional bound morpheme, expressing the subjective doubt regarding a statement. It is postposed to the interrogative pronouns and adverbs to form a kind of quasi-indefinite pronoun and adverb.

OkOe-cO-e ṅoṅkatE paxaoena bañ disəledea 'who ever crossed by this way I had not recognised'

cele-cOe gErkidiña 'which ever bit me'

oka-cO-ñ hataoa bañ bujhəudareak'kana 'what ever I shall take I cannot understand'

cet'cO-m ləikeda bañ bujhəudareada 'what ever you told I could not follow' *tis-cO-e rORleda* 'when he spoke' (time not exactly known)

Inclusive : /hÕ/ : It is used with the subject NP, object NP and adverb to include those parts of the sentences to which it is added

rakkhos hõ-e darkeda 'even the man-eater ran away'

am hõ-ñ ñElet'mea 'I saw even you'

uniak' hõ idiToraymE 'take away even his (things)'

ar nit hõsetak'ena 'and the dawn approached even by this time'

gapa hõ-haT baṅ durup'a 'even tomorrow the market will not sit'

/hÕ/ in conjunction with the copulative *ar* indicates 'again'.
meaṅ arhÕ haT duRup'a 'day after tomorrow again the market will sit'

Interrogative:

/ki/ (cp. Bengali *ki*) 'what'. In a real question it is optionally used after the subject NP.

apE ki biru bapE calak'kana OR *apE biru bapE calak'kana* 'are you not going to Biru ?'

am ki daka bam gadaoakada OR *am daka bam gadaoakada* 'Have you not eaten up rice ?'

am ki noam Emkiña OR *am noam Emkiña* 'Would you give me this ?'

am ki darem mak'leda OR *am darem mak'leda* 'Had you cut the tree ?'

/cedak'/ : 'why'

cedak' birtEpE cȧlak'a 'why do/will you go to the forest?'

cedak'-em landaeda 'why are you laughing ?'

Adverbial : All the particles cited under this category are bound morphemes being incorporated within the verb and thus modifying it.

/tora/ : In conjunction with the verbroot it expresses that something occurs immediately preceding the leaving of a certain place.

uniak' jinis idi-tora-ymE 'take away his thing'

/bara/ : It expresses frequency and habit of certain action.

ñir-baraykanae 'he runs about'

ñutrE alom dǝ R-bara-ya 'do not run about in the darkness'

/OTO/ /hOTO/ : It conveys the idea of the actor departing after having performed any action. /oTo/ is used in the Northern dialect while /hOTO/ is in the Southern.

N.S. *uni khEtrE sare Er-oTo-keda* 'he applied fertilizer in the field'

N.S. *nui gidrǝ dO jãhãsEn idi-oTo-kaemE* 'take away this boy anywhere'

S.S. *uni gidrǝe dOhO-hoTo- keda* 'he put down the child'

S.S. *mErOme tol-hoTo-keda* 'he bound up the goat(for some body)'

/got'/ : It expresses suddenness, instantaneity and quickness of any action.

uni ayo do ǝDie rañgao-gOt'- ena 'his wife suddenly became very angry'

sEn-gOt'-enae 'he went away'

Vocative:

/E / : It is used before kinship terms, names and titles for calling attention.

E pEra	'O friend'
E bOyha	'O brother'
E gO	'O mother'
E mondal	'O Mondal'
E hill dǝi	'O sister-in-law'
E baha mǝi	'O Phulmani'
E yu	'O mother'
E nayke	'O priest'

/ca/ : It is used in addressing younger and inferior ones. It is only used by malefolk.

cet'-ea 'look, what?'

/na/ : It is used after the vocative /E/ and other words by female-folk for calling attention. It is restricted among friends only.

Ena cet' lekarE haTbon calak'a	'look, how shall we go to the market?'
Ena nǝkic' dO alopE bhabnaa	'look, do not worry about comb'

/hEnda/ : It is commonly used by male and female-folk forcalling attention. It may stand alone or may be followed by another particle /ho/.

hEnda baba ona gundli ma bili bele jutəkana 'father, that millet has been ripe'

hEnda ho, gidrəpE ñElkedtiña 'look, did you see my son ?'

/hoi/.

hoi bacha 'o boy'

/rE/ : It is a bound morpheme being added to the person addressed.

dəirE 'O elder sister'

məirE 'O daughter'

dada-rE 'O elder brother'

/go/ : It is used by women.

E yu go 'O mother'

E məi go 'O daughter'

/ho/ : It is used after the words for the persons addressed to call attention.

Morphophonological Change

/baṅ/ may drop its final nasal when the short forms of the personal pronouns are added to it :

baṅ + ñ = bañ

baṅ + e = bae

baṅ + m = bam

The vowel of /baṅ/ is neutralised when the short form of the first personal pronoun is added to it :

baṅ + ñ = [bən]

/coṅ/ drops its final nasal when the short form of the personal pronouns are added to it :

cOṅ + n = coñ

cOṅ + m = cOm

cOṅ + e = cOe

8

CONCLUSION

The analysis affords us to indicate the basic principles in Santali morphology. The morphemes are broadly divided into two groups — roots and non-roots. The roots enter into morphological constructions, while the non-roots do not. The interplay of a root and a non-root is among its most significant features, a mechanism of forming a stem. Functionally roots are classified into nominals, adjectives, adverbs, verbs and particles. The particles are included in this class as they are free like other roots but they are neither inflected nor enter into morphological constructions. The non-roots are invariably bound forms and consist of prefix, infix, suffix and postpositions. The processes employed in the interplay of the morphemes are prefixation, infixation, suffixation, compounding and reduplication. A word is defined as a free root or a root plus a non-root. But longer corpus with reduplication of the whole root or stem with an added suffix is treated as a word as it behaves like a single unit. Such forms are commonly used as adjectives and adverbs.

Santali possesses a large number of derivatives which are mostly derived through infixation and suffixation. The prefixation is limited in use as the prefixes are very small in number. The infixes are mostly inserted into the verb roots to derive a noun. This insertion also takes place in adjectives in a very limited case. Some infixes like /-pV^{r}-/ have dual functions — in derivation they are used to derive noun, e.g. *rapaj* 'king and his retinue' from *raj* 'king', *kipisār* 'zamindar and his retinue' from *kisār* 'zamindar' etc. and in conjugation they are used to form a stem, e.g. *dapal* 'beat each other' from *dal* 'beat', *EpEm* give each other' from *Em* 'give' etc. The compound suffix like /-tEak'/, a compound of the instrumental suffix /-tE/ and impersonal /-ak'/ is used to derive nouns denoting instrumentality. Besides derivation by morphological processes internal derivation plays an important part in morphology.

The animate-inanimate distinction of the nominals is very clear out and affects the whole structure of the language. This distinction is reflected in the choice of suffixes in declension. The nominal declension is carried out with the help of affixes and postpositions as there is no inflexion in Santàli. So it is misleading to say, as mentioned in some of the previous works, there is no declension in Santali. The synthetic character of the language as found in the insertion of the genitive infix within the verb to mark the possessor is being erased by not or less using such method. The infixed genitive is being replaced by the suffixed one. The postpositions are of both indegenous and foreign character. And the foreign ones are phonologically transmuted so sharply that one would easily think them as native ones.

The adjectives and adverbs are either simple roots or combination of morphemes. The reduplicated roots or stems along with suffixes are used as adjectives and adverbs. There longer corpus are used as single units. The grammatical gender is operated in certain adjectives. The degree is affected by the use of postpositions.

The verb occupies a nuclear position in a sentence. The subject and object when animate are shown in the verb. And the mere verb with incorporation of animate subject and/or object can function as a whole sentence. Besides certain action words any word can perform the function of a verb if the suffixes for the tense and aspect are added to it. In this way non-native roots are appended against indegenous verbal suffixes and are treated as verbs. The verbal roots are of three classes — transitive, intransitive and transitive-intransitive. The marker for the transitive is added to the tense/aspect suffixes when added to the roots. The markers for the intransitive are added in the similar fashion. But in the third class the markers for both the classes are used. Like nominal suffixes the verbal suffixes are also not constant i.e. one is not restricted to a particular function, for instance, the suffix/-ok'/ is used for intransitive, passive, reflexive and sometime reciprocal functions. In some cases the phonetic mutation makes it difficult to distinguish between different tenses, as in the simple past and anterior pluperfect with dative and simple past and anterior pluperfect of the benefective.

BIBLIOGRAPHY

Ahmed, Enayat, 1969. Santal Parganas, In : Encyclopaedia Britanica 19, Chicago : William Benton.

Allanson, H. L.L., 1912. Final Report on the Survey and Settlement Operations in the District of Santhal Parganas (Third Programme) 1898-1910, Calcutta : The Bengal Secretariat Book Depot.

Bagchi, P.C., 1929. Pre-Aryan and Pre-Dravidian in India (Translation of articles by S. Levi, J. Przyluski and J. Bloch), Calcutta : University of Calcutta.

Bailey, T. Graham, 1908. Languages of the Northern Himalayas, Asiatic Society Monographs XII, London.

Banerjee, G.C., 1894. Introduction to the Kharia Language, Calcutta : Bengal Secretariat Press.

Banerjee, Manoranjan, 1964. Primitive Men in India, Ambala : The Indian Publications.

Barker, Milton E., 1965. Vietnamese-Muong Tone Correspondences, In Norman H. Zide (ed.) : Studies in Comparative Austroasiatic Linguistics, The Hague : Mouton.

Beams, J., 1971. Outlines of Indian Philology, Calcutta : Firma K.L. Mukhopadhyay.

Bhaduri, M.B., 1931. A Mundari-English Dictionary, Calcutta : Calcutta University.

Bhattacharya, S., 1954. Studies in the Parengi Language, *Indian Linguistics* 14 : III, 45-63.

-----------, 1957. Field-notes on Nahali, *Indian Linguistics* 17, 245-258.

-----------, 1965. Glottal stop and checked consonants in Bonda, *Indian Journal* IX : 1, 69-71.

-----------, 1966. Some Munda Etymologies, In Norman H. Zide (ed.): Studies in Comparative Austroasiatic Linguistics, 28-40, The Hague : Mouton.

-----------, 1968. A Bonda Dictionary, Poona : Deccan College.

-----------, 1969. Some More Munda Etymologies, Poona : Pratidanam.

-----------, 1970. Kinship Terms in the Munda Languages, *Anthropos* 65.

-----------, 1972. Dravidian and Munda, Third Seminar on Dravidian Linguistics, Annamalai University.

-----------, 1975. Munda Studies : A New Classification of Munda, *Indo-Iranian Journal* XVII : 1, 97-101.

Biligiri, H.S. 1965. Kharia : Phonology, Grammar and Vocabulary, Poona : Deccan College.

-----------, 1965. The Sora Verb, A Restricted Study, In G.B. Milner and Eugenie J.A. Henderson (eds.) : Indo-Pacific Linguistic Studies II, 231-250. Amsterdam : North-Holland Publishing Company.

-----------, Biswas, P.C., 1956. Santals of the Santal Parganas, Delhi: Bharatiya Adimjati Sewak Sangha.

Bloch, Bernard and G.L. Trager, 1972. Outlines of Linguistic Analysis, New Delhi : Oriental Books Reprint Corporation.

Bloomfield, L., 1964. Language (Reprint), Delhi : Motilal Banarasidass.

Bodding, P.O., 1922. Materials for a Santali Grammar I (Mostly Phonetic), Dumka : Santal Mission of the Northern Churches.

---------, 1925. Santali Folk Tales 1-3, Oslo : H. Aschehoug & Co.

---------, 1929. Materials For a Santali Grammar II (Mostly Morphological), Dumka : Santal Mission of the Northern Churches.

---------, 1929. A Santali Grammar for Beginners. Bengaria : Santal Mission Press.

----------, 1929-36. A Santal Dictionary 1-5, Oalo : A. W. Broggers Boktrykkeri.

----------, 1942. Traditions and Institutions of the Santals, Oslo : A.W. Broggers Boktrykkeri.

---------, 1955. A Plea for a Standardised System of Writing the Munda or Kolarian Languages, *JASB* (New Series) 21, 9-20.

Bexwell, J. 1887. On the Santali Language, *Transaction of the Philological Society*, London.

Burrows, L. 1915. Ho Grammar, Calcutta : Catholic Orphan Press.

Campbell, A. 1953. Santali-English Dictionary (3rd edn), ed. by R.M. Macphail, Benagaria : Santal Christian Council.

---------, 1954. English-Santali Dictionary (3rd edn), ed. by R.M. Macphail. Benagaria : Santal Christian Council.

Campbell, Sir George, 1874. Specimens of Languages of India, Calcutta : Bengal Secretariat Press.

Campbell, Mr. Justice, 1866. The Ethnology of India, *JASB* (Supplementary No.) XXXV : II, 1-152.

Chakrabarti, M. and D. Mukherji, 1971. Indian Tribes, Calcutta : Saraswat Press.

Chatterji, S.K., 1923. The Study of Kol, *The Calcutta Review* VIII, 451-473.

-------, 1926. The Origin and Development of the Bengali Language, Calcutta : Calcutta University.

-------, 1936. Non-Aryan Elements in Indo-Aryan, *Journal of the Greater India Society* III, 43-49.

-------, 1953. The Languages of the Adivasis. *March in India* 6 : 2, 14-16.

-------, 1961. Foreward to HOR BAPLA PUTHI (pahil hatin) of Stephen H. Murmu, V - XI, Benagaria : Mission Press.

Chowdhuri, N.C., 1977. Munda Social Structure, Calcutta : Firma K.L. Mukhopadhyay.

Cole, Rev. F.T., 1875. Santali Riddles, *Indian Antiquary* IV, 164f.

---------, 1879. List of Words and Phrases with their Santali Equivalents, *Indian Antiquary* VIII, 194-196.

---------, 1906. Santali Primar, Pokhuria : Santal Mission Press.

Cook, Walter A., 1965. A Descriptive Analysis of Mundari : A Study of Structure, Ph.D. Dissertation. Georgetown University.

Dalton, E.T., 1866. The "Kols" of Chota-Nagpur, *JASB* XXIV : III, 153-198.

--------, 1872. Descriptive Ethnology of Bengal, Calcutta : Superintendent, Govt. Printing Press.

Dasgupta, Dipankar, 1978. Linguistic Studies, Calcutta : Anthropological Survey of India.

Datta Majumdar, Nabendu, 1956. The Santal — A Study in Culture Change. Delhi : Anthropoligical Survey of India.
Drake, John, 1903. Grammar of the Kurku Language, Calcutta : Baptist Mission Press.
Ghosh, A., 1980. Santali Kinship Terminology : A Sociolinguistic Perspective, *Calcutta Papers in Linguistics* I : 1, 7-23.
-------- 1980. Some Notable Findings in Santali as compared with that of Bodding (1929), In : Souvenir XI All India Conference of Dravidian Linguists, Hyderabad : Osmania University.
Gleason, H.A., 1979. An Introduction to Descriptive Linguistics (Revised edn), Calcutta : Oxford & IBH Publishing Co.
Greenberg, J. H., 1978. Generalizations About Numeral Systems, In Self (ed.) : Universals of Human Languages, 249-295, Stanford, California : Stanford University Press.
Grierson, G.A., 1906. Linguistic Survey of India, IV ed. by Sten Konow, Calcutta. : Superintendent of Govt. Printing.
Gumperz, J. and H.S. Biligiri, 1957. Notes on the Phonology of Mundari, *Indian Linguistics* XVII, 6-15.
Harris, Zellig S., 1960. Structural Linguistics, Chicago : University of Chicago Press.
Hodgson, B.H., 1848. The Aborigins of Central India, *JASB* XVII : II, 550-558.
Hoffmann, Rev. J., 1903. Encyclopaedia Mundarica, Patna : Superintendent, Govt. Printing Press.
Hunter, W.W., 1868. A Comparative Dictionary of the Languages of India and High Asia, London : Trübner & Co.
--------, 1965. The Annals of Rural Bengal, Calcutta : Indian Studies: Past and Present.
Jesperson, O., 1924. The Philosophy of Grammar, London : George Allen and Unwin Ltd.
Konow, Sten, 1904. Mundas and Dravidas, *The Indian Antiquary*, 33, 121-125.
Kuiper, F.B.J., 1962. Nahali — A Comparative Study, *Mededelingen der koninklijke Nederlandse Akademie Ven Wentenschappen* 25, 239-352.
-----------, 1965. Consonant Variation in Munda, In G.B. Milner and Eugenie J.A. Henderson (ed.) : Indo-Pacific Linguistic Studies I, 54-87, Amsterdam : North-Holland Publishing Co.
Kuritowicz, J., 1936. Derivation Lexicale et Derivation Syntaxique, *Bulletin de la Society de Linguistics de Paris* 37, 79-92.

Lees, R.B., 1960. The Grammar of English Nominalization, The Hague : Mouton.

Luce, G.H., 1965. Danaw, A Dying Austroasiatic language, In G.B. Milner and Eugenie J.A. Henderson (ed) : Indo-Pacific Linguistic Studies I, 98-129. Amsterdam : North-Holland Publishing Co.

Lyall, Sir A.J., 1868. Report on the Ethnological Committee on Papers laid before them, and upon Examination of specimens of Aboriginal Tribes brought to Jubbalpur Exhibition of 1866-67 of Nagpur.

Macphail, R.M., 1935. Notes on Santals, In : Census of India 1931, 1: III, Simla : Govt. of India Press.

--------, 1983. An Introduction to Santali (Reprint), Calcutta : Firma K.L. Mukhopadhyay.

Mahapatra, K. and Zide, N.H., 1972 GTA: Nominal Combining Forms, *Indian Linguistics* 33 : 3, 179-202.

Malkial, Yakov, 1966. Genetic Analysis of Word Formation, In T.A. (ed.) : Current Trends in Linguistics III, 305-364, The Hague : Mouton.

---------, 1978. Derivational Categories, In J. H. Greenberg (ed.) : Universals of Human Language 3, 125-149, Stanford, California : Stanford University Press.

Man, E.G., 1867. Santhalia and the Sonthals, Calcutta : Gee Wyman & Co.

Marchand, H., 1964. A Set of Criteria for the Establishing of Derivational Relationship between Words Unmarked by Derivational Morphemes. *Indo-germanische Forschungen* 69, 10-19.

Martinet, A., 1964. Elements of General Linguistics, London : Faber & Faber.

Martin, W., 1898. English-Santali Vocabulary, Benares : Medical Hall Press.

Matthews, P. H., 1974. Morphology : An Introduction to the Theory of Word-structure, Cambridge : Cambridge University Press.

McAlpin, M. C., 1981. Report on the Condition of the Sonthals ... (Reprint), Calcutta : Firma K.L. Mukhopadhyay.

Mitchell, Rev. M., 1875. Santali Songs with Translations, *Indian Antiquary* IV, 34f.

Mitra, A, 1953. The Tribes and Castes of West Bengal. In : Census of India 1951 (West Bengal), Calcutta : West Bengal Govt. Press.

Munda, R., 1969. Aspects of Mundari Verbs, *Indian Linguistics* 30 : 2, 27-49.

Nida, E.A., 1947. Field Techniques, *International Journal of American Linguistics* 13, 138-146.

--------, 1949. Morphology — The Descriptive Analysis of Words, Ann Arber : The University of Michigan Press.

Nigam, R.C. & D. Dasgupta, 1964. Mundari and the Speech of the Bhumdj— A Study in Bilingualism. *Bulletin of the Anthropological Survey of India* XIII, 163-198.

Palmer, F., 1978. Grammar, Great Britain : E. L.B.S.

Pennanen, E.V., 1972. Current Views of Word-Formation. *Neuphilologische Mitteilungen* 73, 292-308.

Pe, Hla., 1965. A Re-examination of Burmese Classifiers, In G.B. Milner and Eugenie J.A. Handerson (ed.) : Indo-Pacific Linguistic Studies, 163-185, Amsterdam : North-Holland Publishing Co.

Philips, J., 1845. A Santali Primer, Calcutta : School Book Society.

--------, 1850. Sequel to A Santali Primer, Calcutta : School Book Society.

--------, 1852. An Introduction to the Santal Language, Calcutta : Calcutta Book Society.

Pinnow, H.J., 1959. *Versuch einer historischen Lautlehre der Khans-Sprache*, Wiesbaden : Otto-Harrassowits.

--------, 1960. *Uber den Ursprung der voneinander abweichanden Strukturen der Munda-uni Khmer-Nikopar-Sorachon*, *Indo-Iranian Journal* IV, Sl.- 103.

----------, 1965. Personal Pronouns in the Austroasiatic Languages : A Historical Study, In G.B. Milner and Eugenie J.A. Henderson (ed) : Indo-Pacific Linguistic Studies I, 3-42, Amsterdam : North-Holland Publishing Co.

--------, 1963. The Position of the Munda Languages Within the Austroasiatic Language Family, In H.L. Shorto (ed.) : Linguistic Comparison in South East Asia and the Pacific, 140-52.

--------, 1966. A Comparative Study of the Verb in the Munda Language, In Norman H. Zide (ed.) : Studies in Comparative Austroasiatic Linguistic, 96-103, The Hague : Mouton.

Puxley, Rev. E.L., 1868. A Vocabulary of the Santhali Language, London : W. M. Watts.

Risley, H.H., 1891. The Tribes and Castes of Bengal, Calcutta : The Bengal Secretariat Press.

Robins, R. H., 1964. General Linguistics : An Introductory Survey, London : Longmans.

Sebeok, T.A., 1942. An Examination of the Austroasiatic Language Family, *Language* XVIII : III, 206-217.

---------, 1943. The Phonemic System of Santali, *Journal of the American Oriental Society* 63, 66-68.

Shaffer, Robert, 1940. Nahali, Linguistic Study of Palecethnography, *Harvard Journal of Asian Studies* 5, 346- 371.

Skrefsrud, L.O., 1873. A Grammar of the Santhal Language, Benaras: Medical Hall Press.

———, 1887. The Traditions and Institutions of the Santhals, Horkoren mare hapramkoreak' kaths, Bernagaria : Santal Mission Press.

Soren, D., 1976. Santal Sab. Howrah : Santal Language Advancement Board.

Stampe, David, 1965-66. Recent Work on Munda Linguistics I-IV. *IJAL* 31, 332-341; 32, 74-80, 164-168, 390-397.

Starosta, Stanley., 1967. Sora Syntax, Ph.D. Dissertation, University of Wisconsin.

----------, 1971. Derivation and Case in Sora Verbs, *Indian Linguistics* 32 : 3, 194-206.

Tea Districts Labour Association, 1929. Language Handbook Santali, Calcutta : Catholic Orphan Press.

Zide, Arlene K., 1978. A Note on Glottalisation and Release in Munda, *Indian Linguistics* 39 : 1 - 4 (P.B. Pandit), 70-75.

---------, and Zide, N.H., 1975. Semanantic Reconstructions in Proto-Munda Cultural Vocabulary I., *Indian Linguistics* 54 : 1, 1 - 24.

Zide, N. H., 1958. Final Stops in Korku and Santali, *Indian Linguistics* I, 44-48 (Turner).

---------, 1965. Gutob-Remo Vocalism and Glottalised Vowels in Proto-Munda, In G.B. Milner and Eugenie J.A. Henderson (ed.): Indo-Pacific Linguistic Studies I, 43-53. Amsterdam : North- Holland Publishing Co.

---------, 1966. Low Tone and the Proto-Korku-Kherwarian Vowel System, In Self (ed.) : Studies in Comparative Austroasiatic Linguistics, 214-229, The Hague : Mouton.

---------, 1969. Munda and Non-Munda Austroasiatic Languages, In T.A. Sebeok (ed.) : Current Trends in Linguistics 5, 411-433, The Hague : Mouton.

---------, 1976. Studies in the Munda Numerals, Mysore : Central Institute of Indian Languages.

INDEX